PENGUIN BOOKS

COLLECTED POEMS

Roger McGough is one of Britain's best-known poetry voices. Following the success of the bestselling Penguin collection *The Mersey Sound* (with Brian Patten and the late Adrian Henri), he has been captivating children and adults alike with his unique blend of heart and wit for more than four decades. Much travelled and translated, he is now an international ambassador for poetry and was awarded an OBE for his work in 1997. In 2001 he was honoured with the Freedom of the City of Liverpool.

Collected Poems

Roger McGough

PENGUIN BOOKS

PENGUIN BOOKS

Published by the Penguin Group
Penguin Books Ltd, 80 Strand, London WC2R ORL, England
Penguin Group (USA Inc., 375 Hudson Street, New York, New York 10014, USA
Penguin Books Australia Ltd, 250 Camberwell Road, Camberwell, Victoria 3124, Australia
Penguin Books Canada Ltd, 10 Alcorn Avenue, Toronto, Ontario, Canada M4V 3B2
Penguin Books India (P) Ltd, 11 Community Centre, Panchsheel Park, New Delhi – 110 017, India
Penguin Group (NZ), cnr Airborne and Rosedale Roads, Albany, Auckland 1310, New Zealand
Penguin Books (South Africa) (Pty) Ltd, 24 Sturdee Avenue, Rosebank 2196, South Africa

Penguin Books Ltd, Registered Offices: 80 Strand, London WC2R ORL, England

www.penguin.com

First published by Viking 2003
Published in Penguin Books 2004

11

Set by Rowland Phototypesetting Ltd, Bury St Edmunds, Suffolk
Printed in England by Clays Ltd, St Ives plc

A. M. D. G.

ISBN-13: 978-0-141-01455-5

www.greenpenguin.co.uk

Penguin Books is committed to a sustainable future
for our business, our readers and our planet.
The book in your hands is made from paper
certified by the Forest Stewardship Council.

CONTENTS

PREFACE

The poems in this volume represent a span of over forty years, the earliest having been written in my twenties. I decided against a strict chronological order, preferring to bring together those related by theme or genre. Some poems that appeared in *Watchwords* (Cape, 1969) were occasional pieces commissioned for television performance, and in their best interests I have omitted them.

A number of poems have been revised, but only where the language seemed unwieldy, even at the time of writing, and some puns have not improved with age. But I have tried to resist the temptation to revise my original thoughts and feelings, however naive and indiscreet they appear in grizzled retrospect.

Sky in the Pie (Kestrel, 1989) was my first book of poems written for children, and to date there have been six more. The line that divides children's poems from adults' is a blurred one, and the few that have crossed over into this collection seem more at home. It is not a question of their having been upgraded. Seven previously unpublished poems are also included at no extra cost to the reader.

My thanks to Tony Lacey at Penguin, Adrian Mealing at U.K.touring, and to Peters, Fraser & Dunlop, but especially to all the readers and listeners who have supported me over the years.

Learning to Read

Learning to read during the war
wasn't easy, as books were few
and far between. But Mother
made sure I didn't go to sleep
without a bedtime story.

Because of the blackout
the warm, comforting glow
of a bedside lamp was not permitted.
So Mum would pull back the curtains
and open wide the window.

And by the light of a blazing factory
or a crashed Messerschmitt,
cuddled up together, she would read
saucebottles, jamjars, and, my
all-time favourite, a tin of Ovaltine.

So many years ago, but still
I remember her gentle guidance
as I read aloud my first sentence:
'S-p-r-i-n-k-l-e t-w-o h-e-a-p-e-d
t-e-a-s-p-o-o-n-s-f-u-l o-f . . .

My Little Eye

The cord of my new dressing-gown
he helps me tie

Then on to my father's shoulder
held high

The world at night with my little eye
I spy

The moon close enough to touch
I try

Silver painted elephants have learned
to fly

Giants fence with searchlights
in the sky

Too soon into the magic shelter
he and I

Air raids are so much fun
I wonder why

In the bunk below, a big boy
starts to cry.

Bye Bye Black Sheep

Volunteering at seventeen, Uncle Joe
Went to Dunkirk as a Royal Marine
And lived, not to tell the tale.
Demobbed, he brought back a broken 303,
A quiver of bayonets, and a kitbag
Of badges, bullets and swastikas
Which he doled out among warstruck nephews.

With gasflame-blue eyes and dark unruly hair
He could have been God's gift. Gone anywhere.
But a lifetime's excitement had been used up
On his one-and-only trip abroad. Instead,
Did the pools and horses. 'Lash me, I'm bored,'
He'd moan, and use language when Gran
Was out of the room. He was our hero.

But not for long. Apparently he was
No good. Couldn't hold down a job.
Gave the old buck to his Elders and Betters.
Lazy as sin, he turned to drink
And ended up marrying a Protestant.
A regular black sheep was Uncle Joe.
Funny how wrong kids can be.

Snipers

When I was kneehigh to a tabletop,
Uncle Ted came home from Burma.
He was the youngest of seven brothers
so the street borrowed extra bunting
and whitewashed him a welcome.

All the relations made the pilgrimage,
including us, laughed, sang, made a fuss.
He was as brown as a chairleg,
drank tea out of a white mug the size of my head,
and said next to nowt.

But every few minutes he would scan
the ceiling nervously, hands begin to shake.
'For snipers,' everyone later agreed,
'A difficult habit to break.'

Sometimes when the two of us were alone,
he'd have a snooze after dinner
and I'd keep an eye open for Japs.
Of course, he didn't know this
and the tanner he'd give me before I went
was for keeping quiet,
but I liked to think it was money well spent.

Being Uncle Ted's secret bodyguard
had its advantages, the pay was good
and the hours were short, but even so,
the novelty soon wore off, and instead,
I started school and became an infant.

Later, I learned that he was in a mental home.
'Needn't tell anybody . . . Nothing serious
. . . Delayed shock . . . Usual sort of thing
. . . Completely cured now the doctors say.'
The snipers came down from the ceiling
but they didn't go away.

Over the next five years they picked off
three of his brothers; one of whom was my father.
No glory, no citations,
Bang! straight through the heart.

Uncle Ted's married now, with a family.
He doesn't say much, but each night after tea,
he still dozes fitfully in his favourite armchair.
He keeps out of the sun, and listens now and then
for the tramp tramp tramp of the Colonel Bogeymen.
He knows damn well he's still at war,
just that the snipers aren't Japs anymore.

Bucket

everyevening after tea
grandad would take his bucket for a walk

An empty bucket

When i asked him why
he said because it was easier to carry
than a full one

grandad had an answer for everything

Smart Railings

towards the end of his tether
grandad
at the drop of a hat
would paint the railings

overnight
we became famous
allover the neighbourhood
for our smart railings

(and our dirty hats)

Tramp Tramp Tramp

Insanity left him when he needed it most.
Forty years at Bryant & May, and a scroll
To prove it. Gold lettering, and a likeness
Of the Founder. Grandad's name writ small:
'William McGarry, faithful employee'.

A spent match by the time I knew him.
Choking on fish bones, talking to himself,
And walking round the block with a yardbrush
Over his shoulder. 'What for, Gran?' 'Hush . . .
Poor man, thinks he's marching off to war.

'Spitting image of Charlie, was your Grandad,
And taller too.' She'd sigh. 'Best-looking
Man in Seaforth. And straight-backed?
Why, he'd walk down Bridge Road
As if he had a coat-hanger in his suit.'

St Joseph's Hospice for the Dying, in Kirkdale,
Is where Chaplin made his last movie.
He played Grandad, and gave a fine performance
Of a man raging against God, and cursing
The nuns and nurses who tried to hold him down.

Insanity left him when he needed it most.
The pillow taken from his face
At the moment of going under. Screaming
And fighting to regain the years denied,
His heart gave out, his mind gave in, he died.

The final scene brings tears to everybody's eyes.
In the parlour, among suppurating candles
And severed flowers, I see him smiling
Like I'd never seen him smile before.
Coat-hanger at his back. Marching off to war.

Bars are Down

When I was a lad
most people round our way
were barzydown.

It was a world full of piecans.
Men who were barmy, married to women
who wanted their heads examined.

When not painting the railings,
our neighbours were doolally,
away for slates.

Or so my dad reckoned.
Needed locking away
the lot of them.

Leaving certain McGoughs
and a few close friends
free to walk the empty streets

in peace. Knowing exactly
whether we were coming or going.
Self-righteous in polished shoes.

Picking our way
clearheadedly,
between loose screws.

Sad Aunt Madge

As the cold winter evenings drew near
Aunt Madge used to put extra blankets
over the furniture, to keep it warm and cosy.
Mussolini was her lover, and life
was an outoffocus rosy-tinted spectacle.

but neurological experts
with kind blueeyes
and gentle voices
small white hands
and large Rolls Royces
said that electric shock treatment
should do the trick
it did . . .

today after 15 years of therapeutic tears
and an awful lot of ratepayers' shillings
down the hospital meter
sad Aunt Madge
no longer tucks up the furniture
before kissing it goodnight
and admits
that her affair with Mussolini
clearly was not right
particularly in the light
of her recently announced engagement
to the late pope.

Hearts and Flowers

                              Aunty Marge,
Spinster of the parish, never had a boyfriend.
Never courted, never kissed.
A jerrybuilt dentist and a smashed jaw
Saw to that.

To her,
Life was a storm in a holy-water font
Across which she breezed
With all the grace and charm
Of a giraffe learning to windsurf.

But sweating
In the convent laundry, she would iron
Amices, albs and surplices
With such tenderness and care
You'd think priests were still inside.

Deep down,
She would like to have been a nun
And talked of missing her vocation
As if it were the last bus home:
'It passed me by when I was looking the other way.'

'Besides,'
She'd say, 'What Order would have me?
The Little Daughters of the Woodbine?
The Holy Whist Sisters?' A glance at the ceiling.
'He's not that hard up.'

We'd laugh
And protest, knowing in our hearts that He wasn't.
But for the face she would have been out there,
Married, five kids, another on the way.
Celibacy a gift unearned, unasked for.

But though
A goose among grown-ups,
Let loose among kids
She was an exploding fireworks factory,
A runaway pantomime horse.

Everybody's
Favourite aunt. A cuddly toy adult
That sang loud and out of tune.
That dropped, knocked over and bumped into things,
That got ticked off just like us.

                  Next to
A game of cards she liked babysitting best.
Once the parents were out of the way
It was every child for itself. In charge,
Aunt Marge, renegade toddler-in-chief.

                Falling
Asleep over pontoon, my sister and I,
Red-eyed, would beg to be taken to bed.
'Just one more game of snap,' she'd plead,
And magic two toffees from behind an ear.

             Then suddenly
Whooshed upstairs in the time it takes
To open the front door. Leaving us to possum,
She'd tiptoe down with the fortnightly fib:
'Still fast asleep, not a murmur all night. Little angels.'

               But angels
Unangelic, grew up and flew away. And fallen,
Looked for brighter toys. Each Christmas sent a card
With kisses, and wondered how she coped alone.
Up there in a council flat. No phone.

              Her death
Was as quick as it was clumsy. Neighbours
Found the body, not us. Sitting there for days
Stiff in Sunday best. Coat half-buttoned, hat askew.
On her way to Mass. Late as usual.

              Her rosary
Had snapped with the pain, the decades spilling,
Black beads trailing. The crucifix still
Clenched in her fist. Middle finger broken.
Branded into dead flesh, the sign of the cross.

            From the missal
In her lap, holy pictures, like playing cards,
Lay scattered. Five were face-up:
A Full House of Sacred Hearts and Little Flowers.
Aunty Marge, lucky in cards.

Casablanca

You must remember this
To fall in love in Casablanca
To be the champion of Morocco.

The size of tuppence
Photographs show Uncle Bill holding silver cups
Wearing sepia silks and a George Formby grin.

Dominique
Had silent film star looks. With brown eyes
Black hair and lips full to the brim, she was a race apart.

He brought her over
To meet the family early on. An exotic bloom
In bleak post-war Bootle. Just the once.

Had there been children
There might have been more contact. But letters,
Like silver cups, were few and far between.

At seventy-eight
It's still the same old story. Widowed and lonely
The prodigal sold up and came back home.

I met him that first Christmas
He spoke in broken scouse. Apart from that
He looked like any other bow-legged pensioner.

He had forgotten the jockey part
The fight for love and glory had been a brief episode
In a long, and seemingly, boring life.

It turned out
He had never felt at home there
Not a week went by without him thinking of Liverpool.

Casablanca
The airplane on the runway. She in his arms.
Fog rolling in from the Mersey. As time goes by.

What Happened to Henry

What happened to Henry Townsend that summer
still turns my stomach. Not long after the war
when barrage balloons had been cut loose
and coal was delivered by horse and cart

lads would chase the wagon up the street
and when the coalie wasn't looking
grab hold of the tailboard, and legs dangling
hang there for as long as they could.

According to one, Henry, head thrown back
and swinging too close to the edge,
had caught his foot between the spokes
of the rear left wheel. As it turned

his leg snapped in half. I heard the screams
three streets away. Not his, but his mother's,
who'd been gabbing on the corner.
Air-raid sirens to send us all scurrying.

The driver, ashen-faced beneath the coaldust
held fast the reins to prevent the horse
from moving, but nervous, it bucked
and strained and tried to pull away.

Glad to be of use, two men unbuckled the traces,
freed the horse and laid the shafts gently down.
A kitchen chair was brought out so that
Henry could take the weight off his leg.

*   *   *

Those are the facts and this is the picture:
Late one summer's afternoon in Seaforth
on a wooden chair on a cobbled street
a ten-year-old sits with his leg in a wheel.

His mother is crying, but not Henry.
He is stock-still. Against her blue pinny
his face has the pale luminescence of an angel.
A neighbour brings him out a drink of water,

cup and saucer, best china. No sign yet
of an ambulance. Not a policeman in sight.
Frantic, my gran arrives to chase me home.
(Compared to his sister, though, Henry got off light.)

What Happened to Dorothy

That's me on the left.
Page-boy in a velvet suit.
Four years old, blond curls and scowling.
Lucky horseshoe trailing.

That's Dorothy, Maid-of-Honour.
Though only three years older,
in her long white dress,
veil and floral tiara
she could be a teenager.

She never would be, though.

(It wasn't a road accident)
    Tin bath in the kitchen.
(It wasn't diphtheria)
    Pan after pan of boiling water.
(Or polio, or cancer)
    Kids warned not to run about.
(It wasn't murder on the sand dunes)
    Only half full, but scalding
(It wasn't drowning in the canal)
    When she tripped and fell in.

That's me on the left.
Lucky horseshoe still trailing.
That's Dorothy, still seven.

The Fallen Birdman

The oldman in the cripplechair
Died in transit through the air
And slopped into the road.

The driver of the lethallorry
Trembled out and cried: 'I'm sorry,
But it was his own fault.'

Humans snuggled round the mess
In masochistic tenderness
As raindrops danced in his womb.

*   *   *

But something else obsessed my brain,
The canvas, twistedsteel and cane,
His chair, spreadeagled in the rain,
Like a fallen birdman.

Alphabet Soup

Whenever I went into our local library
I would take out a book for my dad.
An adventure yarn. Something to do with the sea.

Occasionally, I'd bring home one he'd read before.
'Doesn't matter,' he would say, 'it's a good 'un.'
And settling down, sign on for the same voyage.

It wasn't laziness on his part, but a kind of fear.
Libraries were for educated people.
Full of traps. Procedures. Forms to fill in.

They would notice his handwriting wasn't joined up
So then they would try and catch him out.
Ask questions about Shakespeare. About proper books.

*   *   *

Although a stevedore (Mum preferred that to 'docker')
And landlubbered all his married life
He'd have passed four-square on seamanship.

Because he'd been to sea himself when young
And would often talk, with some regret,
Of how he'd nearly jumped ship in Fremantle.

He loved the solitude of the bush. Its stillness,
And the sky a blueprint for eternity.
'And the names of the places. Now that's poetry!'

I picture ourselves in the outback
The nearest library five hundred miles away
Him, married to a girl from Manjimup
Me, trying to make sense of alphabet soup.

The Railings

You came to watch me playing cricket once.
Quite a few of the fathers did.
At ease, outside the pavilion
they would while away a Saturday afternoon.
Joke with the masters, urge on
their flannelled offspring. But not you.

Fielding deep near the boundary
I saw you through the railings.
You were embarrassed when I waved
and moved out of sight down the road.
When it was my turn to bowl though
I knew you'd still be watching.

Third ball, a wicket, and three more followed.
When we came in at the end of the innings
the other dads applauded and joined us for tea.
Of course, you had gone by then. Later,
you said you'd found yourself there by accident.
Just passing. Spotted me through the railings.

* * *

Speech-days • Prize-givings • School-plays
The Twentyfirst • The Wedding • The Christening
You would find yourself there by accident.
Just passing. Spotted me through the railings.

Squaring Up

When I was thirteen and crimping my first quiff
Dad bought me a pair of boxing-gloves
In the hope that I would aspire to the Noble Art.

But I knew my limitations from the start:
Myopia, cowardice and the will to come second.
But I feigned enthusiasm for his sake.

Straight after tea, every night for a week
We would go a few rounds in the yard.
Sleeves rolled up, collarless and gloveless

He would bob and weave and leave me helpless.
Uppercuts would tap me on the chin
Left hooks muss my hair, haymakers tickle my ear.

Without glasses, only one thing was clear:
The fact that I was hopeless. He had a son
Who couldn't square up. So we came to blows.

Losing patience, he caught me on the nose.
I bled obligingly. A sop. A sacrifice.
Mum threw in the towel and I quit the ring.

But when the bell goes each birthday I still feel the sting
Not of pain, but of regret. You said sorry
And you were. I didn't. And I wasn't.

'What does your father do?'

At university, how that artful question embarrassed me.
In the common-room, coffee cup balancing on cavalry twills
Some bright spark (usually Sociology) would want an answer.
Shame on me, as feigning lofty disinterest, I would hesitate.

Should I mumble 'docker' in the hope of being misheard?
('There he goes, a doctor's son, and every inch the medical man.')
Or should I pick up the hook and throw it down like a gauntlet?
'Docker. My dad's a docker.' A whistle of corduroy.

How about? 'He's a stevedore, from the Spanish "estibador"
Meaning a packer, or loader, as in ship.' No, sounds too
On the Waterfront, and Dad was no Marlon Brando.
Besides, it's the handle they want not the etymology.

'He's a foreman on the docks.' A hint of status? Possibly.
A touch of class? Hardly. Better go with the straightforward:
'He works on the docks in Liverpool,' which leaves it open.
Crane-driver? Customs and Excise Officer? Canteen manager?

Clerk? Chairman of the Mersey Docks and Harbour Board?
In dreams, I hear him naming the docks he knew and loved.
A mantra of gentle reproach: *Gladstone, Hornby, Alexandra,*
Langton, Brocklebank, Canada, Huskisson, Sandon, Wellington,

Bramley Moor, Nelson, Salisbury, Trafalgar, Victoria.

Having My Ears Boxed

I am waiting in the corridor
To have my ears boxed.
I am nervous, for Mr O'Hanlon
Is a beast of his word.

For the last twenty minutes
I have let my imagination
Run away with itself.
But I am too scared to follow.

Will he use that Swiss Army knife
To slice through cleanly? Bite them off?
Tear carefully along perforated lines?
Tug sharply like loose Elastoplasts?

Acknowledging the crowd's roar
Will he hold my head aloft
As if it were the FA Cup
And pull the handles? Aagghhrr . . .

And then the box. Cardboard?
Old cigar-box possibly? Or a pair?
Separate coffins of polished pine.
L and R. 'Gone to a better place.'

Impatient now, I want to get it
Over with. Roll on four o'clock.
When, hands over where-my-ears-used-to-be
I run the gauntlet of jeering kids.

At six, mother arrives home weary
After a hard day at the breadcrumb factory.
I give her the box. She opens it
And screams something. I say:

'Pardon?'

Another Brick in the Wall

'Its like bashing your head against a brick wall,'
said Brother Ryan,
bashing my head against a brick wall.

Sacrifices

I was forever hearing about the sacrifices
My parents made.
Little ones almost daily
Big ones when required.

Having me meant sacrifices. Going without.
And then to cap it all, the Scholarship:
School uniforms, violin lessons,
Elocution, extra tuition.

'If it's not one thing it's another.
I hope you're worth it.' But was I?
The dictionary confirmed my doubts:
'*Sacrifice*, a ritual killing of a person
or animal with the intention of pleasing a deity.'

Sacrifice. No, I wasn't worth it.
All that blood for a few O-levels.

Wearing Thin

'You'll soon grow into it,' she would say
When buying a school blazer three sizes too big.
And she was right as mothers usually are.

Syrup of figs. Virol. Cod liver oil.
Within a year I did grow into it
By then, of course, it was threadbare.

Pulling in different directions
My clothes and I never matched.
And in changing-rooms nothing has changed.

I can buy what I like and when
New clothes that are a perfect fit.
Full-length mirror, nervous grin,
It's me now that's threadbare, wearing thin.

How to Become a Sixer

Wait until Akela is out of the room
and the noise level begins to rise.
As soon as you hear returning footsteps
call out in a loud, clear voice:
'Quiet everybody. We promised to get on
with things in silence. DYB. DYB. DYB. Remember?'

By now the footsteps will have stopped
and the Pack looking to see if you are being serious.
Ignore them, and use the pause
to do something useful, like tying a knot.
Akela will then make stamping noises
and open the door. Everything is shipshape.

Acknowledge the appraising glance
but appear embarrassed, as if you wished
you could bite your tongue off.
Promotion will quickly follow. And disappointment:
Akela in a tent, unfurling his knob.
Dirty Old Bugger. DOB. DOB. DOB.

Maurice

There were no 'gays' in those days, only 'funny' men.
Enter Mrs Thomas: 'He's a bit effeminate
That Maurice. "Funny", if you ask me.

Bringing his "friend" home on leave
The two of them in bed and her bringing in the tea.
His own mother not knowing. It will end in tears.

What do they call themselves nowadays?
Course, she brought it all on herself. (Queers!
That's it.) Spoiled from the word go.

Too nesh to play out in the street.
The other boys were rough, and Ho! Ho!
He might be led astray. Him, led astray?

Mind you, it's none of my business
Live and let live, that's what I say.
Although, to be honest, if I had my way

I'd put the pair of them on show in the zoo.
I mean, what do they see in each other?
I mean, what do they actually, pardon the expression, do?'

Hard Times

(i)

Each year, in early December
Grandma would oblige
by falling over
and dislocating something

In hospital, on Christmas Day
all the family would visit
Sit round the bed
and gobble up her dinner.

(ii)

To eke out extra money
during the summer holidays
my schoolfriends and I
would go nit-picking

Conditions were terrible
and the pay was poor
But there were perks:
We were allowed to keep the eggs.

If we could have afforded a bath
We would have had the best. A fine one.
Iron. Broad as a bed, deep as the ocean.
Standing in wingèd feet, proud as a lion.

And oh, what coal we would have stored in it.
Nuggets, big as babies' heads, still blinking
In the daylight. Black as wedding-boots,
So polished you could see your face in them.

And oh, what stories we might have told,
Seated round the hearth on winter nights
The fire crackling, the flames leaping,
Amber liquor sparkling in crystal glasses.

Unfortunately, we were too poor to know stories.

Spitting Prohibited

When I was a boy (cue Brass Band)
A notice downstairs on every bus and tram
Said: NO SMOKING, SPITTING PROHIBITED.

Then overnight, or so it seemed, things changed.
The second part was painted over
And the sign said simply: NO SMOKING.

Imagine that first morning, when passengers,
Bleary-eyed, looked up and saw,
By omission, an invitation.

Then did everybody, unrestrained,
Leap up, clear their throats and let rip?
Expectorate to their lungs' content?

Did drip, dribble, spurt and spatter?
Hawk and croak until the windows were streaming
And the passageways awash?

Transport Committee met and unanimously agreed
That every by-law be clearly stated
And the notice then to read:

NO SMOKING. SPITTING PROHIBITED.
PLEASE REFRAIN FROM URINATING AND DEFECATING,
SOLICITING AND IMPORTUNING.

FORNICATION AND BESTIALITY FORBIDDEN.
ARSON, RAPE AND PILLAGE NOT PERMITTED.
(STRICTLY, NO BRASS BANDS.)

Ee Bah Gum

Spare a thought for your grandmother
who would sit me on her knee
(she had just the one), and tell ee
bah gum stories of days gone by.

'Ee bah gum, it were reet tough,'
she would say, 'workin at mill
from dawn until dusk,
and all for a measly ten shillin a week.'

The thought of clogs and cobbled streets
of matchstick men and smoking chimneys
would bring a tear to her eye,
(she had just the one), then, brightening:

'Mind you, in those days you could buy a nice house,
end-of-terrace for sixpence,
and for a fortnight in Blackpool
you got change out of a farthing.'

Spare a thought for your grandmother
who married well and wanted lots
and lots of children (she had just the one),
and so bequeathed to me, her Lowrys.

A Fine Tooth Comb

When granny was young she was famous for her teeth.
Although, not so much for her teeth
as for the thick golden hair that covered them.
Unusual, even for those days.

But that blonde smile was her crowning glory
and last thing at night, she would gargle
with shampoo before combing her teeth,
or brushing with a pocket-sized Mason & Pearson.

They were the pride of Halifax, and many a lad
came a-calling, until Ted. Love at first sight
they were married the following year.
Then came the war and the long march into night.

As granny grew older her teeth fell out
one by one, and her hair turned grey.
And today, she has but a single tooth
set in a thin curtain of silver.

Alone now, but the nightly ritual continues
as she takes from her dressing-table drawer
'A present to my one and only girl'
from Ted who went to war and didn't come home.

Polished rosewood inlaid with pearl:
A fine tooth comb.

Vague Impressions

Ossie Edwards couldn't punch a hole in a wet echo.
He was no fighter.
And if he wasn't thicker than two short planks
he wasn't much brighter.
To compensate, he did impressions.
Impressions of trains, impressions of planes,
of James Cagney and Donald Duck.

As they all sounded the same
his impressions made little impression
on the 3rd year Cosa Nostra
and so he was bullied mercifully.

Then, quite suddenly, Ossie saw the light.
One Monday morning during R.I.
he switched to birdcalls.
Peewits, kestrels, tomtits and kingfishers
he became them all.
Larks and nightingales.
The birdnotes burst from his throat
like a host of golden buckshot.

And as the nearest anyone got to ornithology
was playing football on a debris with a dead pigeon
there could be no argument.
So he was rechristened 'Percy'
and left alone.
And left alone
he twittered his way happily to 3 'O' levels
and a job in a shipping office.

'Twas there he met Sylvia
whom he courted and married.
She took an interest in his hobby
and they were soon appearing in local concerts:
'The Sylvatones – Bird Impressionists'.
The double-act ended however
when Sylvia left him for a widower
who taught her how to sing.
Her love for Perce she realised
never was the real thing,
but, like his impressions, a tuneful imitation.

And that was years ago and still
whenever I pass that way at night
and hear the shrill
yearning hoot of an owl,
I imagine Percy

perched out there in the darkness,
lonely, obsessed.
Calling for his love
to return to the nest.

George and the Dragonfly

Georgie Jennings was spit almighty.
When the golly was good
he could down a dragonfly at 30 feet
and drown a 100 midges with the fallout.
At the drop of a cap
he would outspit lads
years older and twice his size.
Freckled and rather frail
he assumed the quiet dignity
beloved of schoolboy heroes.

But though a legend in his own playtime
Georgie Jennings failed miserably in the classroom
and left school at 15 to work for his father.
And talents such as spitting
are considered unbefitting
for upandcoming porkbutchers.

I haven't seen him since,
but like to imagine some summer soiree
when, after a day moistening mince,
George and his wife entertain tanned friends.
And after dinner, sherrytongued talk
drifts back to schooldays,
the faces halfrecalled, the adventures
overexaggerated. And the next thing
that shy sharpshooter of days gone by
is led, vainly protesting, on to the lawn
where, in the hush of a golden august evening
a reputation, 20 years tall, is put to the test.

So he takes extra care as yesterheroes must,
fires, and a dragonfly, encapsulated, bites the dust.
Then amidst bravos and tinkled applause,
blushing, Georgie leads them back indoors.

Snowing Down South

'It's snowing down south,' one girl would say
When another's petticoat showed beneath the skirt
And, giggling, they would rush off to the Ladies.

Modesty restored, they would return to the floor
And dance demurely, with a poise we could not match
We boys, who stood pretending not to watch.

Then half an hour or so before the Last Waltz
The DJ would put on some rock 'n' roll
And emboldened with ale, we'd form a ring.

Eyes closed, they'd spin, those girls, skirts swirling high
To reveal . . . Need I go on? Mid-fifties.
You've seen the pictures, heard the songs.

In the spotlight of our lascivious gaze
Fired by the rhythm, our whistles and screeches
Down south, suddenly, everything is peaches.

An Apology

Sincere apologies, too late I know, for not getting engaged
on the night we'd planned, Christmas Eve 1962. I had the ring
in my pocket, the one we'd bought together that November
from the little jewellers on Whitefriargate in Hull. Remember?

After Midnight Mass arm-in-arming back to ours,
we linger outside the gates of Seaforth Park. The moon
smiling and expectant. No wind, no people, no cars.
Sheets of ice are nailed to the streets with stars.

The scene is set, two lovers on the silver screen.
A pause, the copy-book kiss. Did angels sing?
This was my moment, the cue to pledge my troth,
to take out the blue, velvet box, and do my stuff.

But marriage was a bridge I feared might be detonated,
And I had this crazy idea that if I didn't mention it, then you
wouldn't either. That we'd collude in romantic amnesia.
That life would go on as before. What could be easier?

Christmas passed. Enraged, you blew up. I felt the blast.
We got engaged. It didn't last.

humdinger

there's not a one

                                        no one
                                        anywhere/place

quite like you

i would follow you to the very ends
of our street

                                        and often do

(discreet-
ly)

                                        onallfours

youra   HUMDINGER

Why, everybody says so

what i wouldn't give for an excursion into your darkest africa.

Man the Barricades, the Enemy has let loose his Pyjamas!

yesterday
secure behind
your barricade
of polite coffeecups
you sat
whittling clichés

but lastnight
slyold me
got you up
some dark alleyway
of my dreams

this morning
you have a   faraway look
in your
smalltalk

Shy

The shy girl at the party
turned out to be

the shy girl in the car
turned out to be

the shy girl in the bedroom
turned out to be

with the light
turned out to be

shyning!

Rainbow

With a rainbow under your arm
you came a-calling.

A home-made cardboard cut-out.
A spangled boomerang. A gift.

That night we put it on the bed.
Made love, a wish, and slept.

(Later, your rainbows would appear
in bedrooms allover town)

With a rainbow under your arm
you came a-calling.

A two-dimensional cartoon of the real thing.
Tongue-in-sky. Our love.

Poem on being in love with two girls at the same time

i have a photograph of you
in the insidepocket of my head
        a blurred photograph
        a double image
is it one girl or is it two?
is it her or is it you?
                Damcamara
                Damcamara

Comeclose and Sleepnow

it is afterwards
and you talk on tiptoe
happy to be part
of the darkness
lips becoming limp
a prelude to tiredness.
Comeclose and Sleepnow
for in the morning
when a policeman
disguised as the sun
creeps into the room
and your mother
disguised as birds
calls from the trees
you will put on a dress of guilt
and shoes with broken high ideals
and refusing coffee
run
alltheway
home.

A lot of Water has Flown under your Bridge

i remember your hands
white and strangely cold
asif exposed too often to the moon

i remember your eyes
brown and strangely old
asif exposed too often and too soon

i remember your body
young and strangely bold
asif exposed too often

i remember
i remember how
when you laughed
hotdogmen allover town
burst into song

i remember
i remember how
when you cried
the clouds cried too and the
streets became awash with tears

i remember
i remember how
when we lay together for the first time
the room smiled,
said: 'excuse-me',
and tiptoed away.

but time has passed since then
and alotof people
have crossed over the bridge
(a faceless throng)

but time has passed since then
and alotof youngmen
have swum in the water
(naked and strong)

but time has passed since then
and alotof water
   has flown
     under
       your
         bridge.

Aren't We All

Looks quite pretty lying there
Can't be asleep yet
Wonder what she's thinking about?
Penny for her thoughts
Probably not worth it.
There's the moon trying to look romantic
Moon's too old that's her trouble
Aren't we all?

Lace curtains gently swaying
Like a woman walking
A woman ina negligee
Walking out through the window
Over the sleeping city up into the sky
To give the moon a rest
Moon's too tired that's her trouble
Aren't we all?

Wasn't a bad party really
Except for the people
People always spoil things
Room's in a mess
And this one's left her clothes allover the place
Scattered like seeds
In too much of a hurry that's her trouble
Aren't we all?

Think she's asleep now
It makes you sleep
Better than Horlicks
Not so pretty really when you get close-up
Wonder what her name is?
Now she's taken all the blankets
Too selfish that's her trouble
Aren't we all?

after the merrymaking, love?

after the merrymaking,
love.
Back to my place
it's not far
a little shedevil
whoever you are.
It was great fun while I lasted.

after the love,
sleep.
In the onrush of its lava
we are caught
side by side
arms entangled
carcass to carcass.

after the sleep,
emptiness.
The sweat dry
and a little nearer death
we awake to meet the day
I pretend it's not goodbye
You pretend you'd love to stay.

The Act of Love

The Act of Love lies somewhere
between the belly and the mind
I lost the love sometime ago
Now I've only the act to grind.

Brought her home from a party
don't bother swapping names
identity's not needed
when you're only playing games.

High on bedroom darkness
we endure the pantomime
ships that go bang in the night
run aground on the sands of time.

Saved in the nick of dawn
it's cornflakes and then goodbye
another notch on the headboard
another day wondering why.

The Act of Love lies somewhere
between the belly and the mind
I lost the love sometime ago
Now I've only the act to grind.

Dunenudes

a pinta makes a man
thats so very true
i know cos i'm a milkman
and my friend is too

a pinta shapes a girl
thats so very true
we found her on a sanddune
the sky a poster blue

milk will soon turn sour
thats so very true
so we lay among the pintas
without anymore ado

the bottles now are broken
the milk has slaked the sand
and we walk into the sunset
hand in hand in hand

My little plastic mac

Teach me, o Lord, to be permissive
the sixties way to save the soul
three leers for sexual freedom
let the good times rock'n'roll.

Tired of being puritan
and living by the code
I learned the New Morality
and shed my guilty load.

I read the kinky magazines
to gain my evil ends
scanned the personal columns
for interesting friends.

And now I've got the taste for sin
I know I'll never stop
just can't wait to get married
so I'll have a wife to swap.

I'm all for divorce and abortion
and the contraceptive pill
let's hear it from the audience
for the homosexual bill.

Here's to the New Morality
pornographers may they thrive
when there's blue films on at the Odeon
it'll be good to be alive.

And once the ball starts rolling
who knows very soon
there'll be a complete set of the Marquis de Sade
in every hotel room.

God bless the new reformers
let them make our island home
a country fit for psychopaths
and nutters like me to roam.

You see at bedtime when I've put away
my flagellation kit
I often shed a silent tear
and I'm forced to admit
that it isn't always easy
being a sexual maniac
as I slide between the rubber sheets
in my little plastic mac.

Discretion

Discretion is the better part of Valerie
though all of her is nice
lips as warm as strawberries
eyes as cold as ice
the very best of everything
only will suffice
not for her potatoes
and puddings made of rice

Not for her potatoes
and puddings made of rice
she takes carbohydrates
like God takes advice
a surfeit of ambition
is her particular vice
Valerie fondles lovers
like a mousetrap fondles mice

And though in the morning
she may whisper: 'it was nice'
you can tell by her demeanour
that she keeps her love on ice
but you've lost your hardearned heart
now you'll have to pay the price
for she'll kiss you on the memory
and vanish in a trice

Valerie is corruptible
but known to be discreet
Valerie rides a silver cloud
where once she walked the street.

Who was the Naughty Girl?

Who was the naughty girl I saw combing her hair with a bluebell
Who was the naughty girl I saw paying her fare with a seashell
Who was the naughty girl I saw sawing the seesaw in two
Who reported Dr Barnardo to the NSPCC
Peter Scott to the RSPB
Who sent the Pope a Playboy key, Jack Ruby a get-well card
The Elephant Man a Valentine card, Pontius Pilate a Xmas card
The Boston Strangler a calling card
Who was the naughty girl who passed Lot the salt
Who went to lunch with William Burroughs, naked
Who fed foie gras to the geese
Who helped the blindman into the ladies
Who snitched on Guy Fawkes
Who switched on Caryl Chessman
Who knitted socks for the Viet Cong
Who was the naughty girl
who put L.S.D. in my Horlicks
Evostick in my contact lenses
Chloroform in my handkerchief
Pig's liver in my pockets
Ants in my gants
Who was the naughty girl?
Why, you.

Contact lenses

Somenights
she leaves them in
until after they have made love.
She likes to see clearly
the lines and curves of bodies.
To watch his eyes, his mouth.
Somenights she enjoys that.

Othernights
when taken by the mood
she takes them out before
and abandons herself
to her blurred stranger.
Other senses compete to compensate.
All is flesh. Looks bigger too.

Near to You

America's the land of milk and honey
Australia's healthy and continually sunny
The living in Sweden is clean and sleek
The food in France is gastronomique

Japan's got geishas and the fastest train
China's got oodles of chicken chow mein
If you want noodles you can't beat Hong Kong's
Brazilians samba on beaches in thongs

Africa looks to a future exciting
Spain's got sherry, el sol and bullfighting
Eskimos are tough and used to roughing
Turkey is full of chestnut stuffing

The Belgians invented the Brussels sprout
Germans lieben lederhosen und sauerkraut
Greece abounds in classical ruins
Russia's violinists play the loveliest tuins

In Bermuda it's swaying palm trees and foam
In Switzerland it's gnome sweet gnome
Italian girls make a di fantastic lovers
Danes are mustard under the covers

From old Hawaii to New Nepal
Foreigners seem to have it all
So if everything abroad is as good as they say
Why do we Britons in Britain stay?

The answer is (and I'm sure it's true)
That all of us want to be near to you

Sundeath/greentears

when you said you loved me
the sun
leapt out from behind st georges hall
and ran around town;

kissing younggirls' faces
    exposing fatmen's braces
    freeing birds & chasing flies
    pulling hats down over eyes
    making bobbies get undressed
    barrowladies look their best
    wayside winos sit and dream
    hotdogmen to sell ice-cream

but when you said goodbye
i heard that the sun
had been runover
somewhere in castle street
by a busload of lovers
whom you have yet to meet

If life's a lousy picture, why not leave before the end

Don't worry
one night we'll find that deserted kinema
the torches extinguished
the cornish ripples locked away in the safe
the tornoff tickets chucked
in the tornoff shotbin
the projectionist gone home to his nightmare

Don't worry
that film will still be running
(the one about the sunset)
& we'll find two horses
tethered in the front stalls
& we'll mount
& we'll ride off
                    into
                our
                    happy
                        ending

You and Your Strange Ways

increasingly oftennow
you reach into your handbag
(the one I bought some xmasses ago)
and bringing forth
a pair of dead cats
skinned and glistening
like the undersides of tongues
or old elastoplasts
sticky with earwigs
you hurl them at my eyes
and laugh cruellongly
why?

even though we have grown older together
and my kisses are little more than functional
i still love you
you and your strange ways

The Fish

you always were a strange girl now weren't you?
like the midsummernights party we went to
where towards witching
being tired and hot of dancing
we slipped thro' the frenchwindows
and arminarmed across the lawn

pausing at the artificial pond
lying liquidblack and limped
in the stricttempo air we kissed
when suddenly you began to tremble
and removing one lavender satin glove knelt
and slipped your hand into the slimy mirror

your face was sad as you brought forth
a switching twitching silver fish
which you lay at my feet
and as the quick tick of the grass
gave way to the slow flop of death
stillkneeling you said softly: 'dont die little fish'

then you tookoff your other glove
and we lay sadly and we made love
as the dancers danced slowly
the fish stared coldly
and the moon admired its reflection
in the lilypetalled pond

May Ball

The evening lay before us
like her silken dress
arranged carefully over the bed.
It would be a night to remember.
We would speak of it often
in years to come. There would
be good food and wine,
cabaret, and music to dance to.
How we'd dance.
How we'd laugh.
We would kiss indiscreetly,
and what are lawns for
but to run barefoot across?

But the evening didn't do
what it was told.
It's the morning after now
and morningafter cold.
I don't know what went wrong
but I blame her. After all
I bought the tickets.
Of course, I make no mention,
that's not my style,
and I'll continue to write
at least for a while.
I carry her suitcase down to the hall,
our first (and her last) University Ball.

The sun no longer loves me

The sun no longer loves me.
When i sit waiting for her
in my little room
she arrives
not cheerfully
but out of a sense of duty
like a National Health prostitute.

Sometimes
she leans silky
against the wall
lolling and stretchy
but mostdays she fidgets
and scratches at clouds.
Whenever i ask her to stay the night
she takes umbrage
and is gone.

Vinegar

sometimes
i feel like a priest
in a fish & chip queue
quietly thinking
as the vinegar runs through
how nice it would be
to buy supper for two

On having no one to write
a love poem about

thismorning
while strolling through my head
rummaging in litterbins
i found by the roadside
an image
that someone had thrown away
A rose

i picked it up
hurried into a backstreet
away from the busy thoroughfare of thoughts
and waited to give it
to the first girl who smiled at me

it's getting dark
and i'm still waiting
The rose attracts a fly

   getting dark
two groupies and a dumb broad
have been the only passersby

       dark
I chance a prayer
There is a smell of tinsel in the air.

My cat and i

Girls are simply the prettiest things
My cat and i believe
And we're always saddened
When it's time for them to leave

We watch them titivating
(that often takes a while)
And though they keep us waiting
My cat & i just smile

We like to see them to the door
Say how sad it couldn't last
Then my cat and i go back inside
And talk about the past.

Dreampoem

in a corner of my bedroom
     grew a tree
     a happytree
     my own tree
its leaves were soft
     like flesh
and its birds sang poems for me
then
     without warning
two men
     with understanding smiles
and axes
     made out of forged excuses
came and chopped it down
either   yesterday
     or the day before
i think it was the day before

Dreampoem 2

I forsake dusty springfield
to follow you out of the theatre.
You are friendly but not affectionate.
I haven't seen you for ages.

You now have a son.
I overhear you telling a stranger
that he is called Menelaus
after the son of my mistress.

I follow you through vast antique shops
where I consider buying a throne.
Instead I go out into the busy road
and under a flyover.
You are nowhere in sight.
The searchlight in the citycentre
is still fingering the sky
though it is now well after midday.

Realizing that I will never see you again
and overwhelmed with whatmighthavebeenness
I give myself up
at the nearest marriage bureau.

What You Are

you are the cat's paw
among the silence of midnight goldfish

you are the waves
which cover my feet like cold eiderdowns

you are the teddybear (as good as new)
found beside a road accident

you are the lost day
in the life of a child murderer

you are the underwatertree
around which fish swirl like leaves

you are the green
whose depths I cannot fathom

you are the clean sword
that slaughtered the first innocent

you are the blind mirror
before the curtains are drawn back

you are the drop of dew on a petal
before the clouds weep blood

you are the sweetfresh grass that goes sour
and rots beneath children's feet

you are the rubber glove
dreading the surgeon's brutal hand

you are the wind caught on barbed wire
and crying out against war

you are the moth
entangled in a crown of thorns

you are the apple for teacher
left in a damp cloakroom

you are the smallpox injection
glowing on the torchsinger's arm like a swastika

you are the litmus leaves
quivering on the suntan trees

you are the ivy
which muffles my walls

you are the first footprints in the sand
on bankholiday morning

you are the suitcase full of limbs
waiting in a leftluggage office
to be collected like an orphan

you are a derelict canal
where the tincans whistle no tunes

you are the bleakness of winter before the cuckoo
catching its feathers on a thornbush
heralded spring

you are the stillness of Van Gogh
before he painted the yellow vortex of his last sun

you are the still grandeur of the *Lusitania*
before she tripped over the torpedo
and laid a world war of american dead
at the foot of the blarneystone

you are the distance
between Hiroshima and Calvary
measured in mother's kisses

you are the distance
between the accident and the telephone box
measured in heartbeats

you are the distance
between power and politicians
measured in half-masts

you are the distance
between advertising and neuroses
measured in phallic symbols

you are the distance
between you and me
measured in tears

you are the moment
before the noose clenched its fist
and the innocent man cried: treason

you are the moment
before the warbooks in the public library
turned into frogs and croaked khaki obscenities

you are the moment
before the buildings turned into flesh
and windows closed their eyes

you are the moment
before the railwaystations burst into tears
and the bookstalls picked their noses

you are the moment
before the buspeople turned into teeth
and chewed the inspector
for no other reason than he was doing his duty

you are the moment
before the flowers turned into plastic and melted
in the heat of the burning cities

you are the moment
before the blindman puts on his dark glasses

you are the moment
before the subconscious begged to be left in peace

you are the moment
before the world was made flesh

you are the moment
before the clouds became locomotives
and hurtled headlong into the sun

you are the moment
before the spotlight moving across the darkened stage
like a crab finds the singer

you are the moment
before the seed nestles in the womb

you are the moment
before the clocks had nervous breakdowns
and refused to keep pace with man's madness

you are the moment
before the cattle were herded together like men

you are the moment
before God forgot His lines

you are the moment of pride
before the fiftieth bead

you are the moment
before the poem passed peacefully away at dawn
like a monarch

A Square Dance

In Flanders fields in Northern France
They're all doing a brand new dance
It makes you happy and out of breath
And it's called the Dance of Death

Everybody stands in line
Everybody's feeling fine
We're all going to a hop
1 – 2 – 3 and over the top

It's the dance designed to thrill
It's the mustard gas quadrille
A dance for men – girls have no say in it
For your partner is a bayonet

See how the dancers sway and run
To the rhythm of the gun
Swing your partner dos-y-doed
All around the shells explode

Honour your partner form a square
Smell the burning in the air
Over the barbed wire kicking high
Men like shirts hung out to dry

If you fall that's no disgrace
Someone else will take your place
'Old soldiers never die . . .'

                                    . . . Only young ones

In Flanders fields where mortars blaze
They're all doing the latest craze
Khaki dancers out of breath
Doing the glorious Dance of Death
Doing the glorious Dance of Death

On Picnics

at the goingdown of the sun
and in the morning
i try to remember them
but their names are ordinary names
and their causes are thighbones
tugged excitedly from the soil
by frenchchildren
on picnics

Why Patriots are a Bit Nuts in the Head

Patriots are a bit nuts in the head
because they wear
red, white and blue-
tinted spectacles
(red for blood
white for glory
and blue . . .
for a boy)
and are in effervescent danger
of losing their lives
lives are good for you
when you are alive
you can eat and drink a lot
and go out with girls
(sometimes if you are lucky
    you can even go to bed with them)

but you can't do this
if you have your belly shot away
and your seeds
spread over some corner of a foreign field
to facilitate
in later years
the growing of oats by some peasant yobbo

when you are posthumous it is cold and dark
and that is why patriots are a bit nuts in the head

M62

The politicians
(who are buying huge cars with hobnailed
   wheels the size of merry-go-rounds)
      have a new plan.
      They are going to
      put cobbles
      in our eyesockets
      and pebbles
      in our navels
      and fill us up
      with asphalt
      and lay us
      side by side
so that we can take a more active part
      in the road
      to destruction.

Noah's Arc

In my fallout shelter I have enough food
For at least three months. Some books,
Scrabble, and games for the children.
Calor gas and candles. Comfortable beds
And a chemical toilet. Under lock and key
The tools necessary for a life after death.
I have carried out my instructions to the letter.

Most evenings I'm down here. Checking the stores,
Our suits, breathing apparatus. Cleaning
And polishing. My wife, bless her,
Thinks I'm obsessive – like other men
About cars or football. But deep down
She understands. I have no hobbies.
My sole interest is survival.

Every few weeks we have what I call D.D.,
Or Disaster Drill. At the sound of the alarm
We each go about our separate duties:
Disconnecting services, switching off the mains,
Filling the casks with fresh water, etc.
Mine is to oversee everything before finally
Shooting the dog. (This I mime in private.)

At first, the young ones enjoyed the days
And nights spent below. It was an adventure.
But now they're at a difficult age
And regard extinction as the boring concern
Of grown-ups. Like divorce and accountancy.
But I am firm. Daddy knows best
And one fine day they'll grow to thank me.

Beneath my bunk I keep an Armalite rifle
Loaded and ready to use one fine day
When panicking neighbours and so-called friends

Try to clamber aboard. The ones who scoff,
Who ignore the signs. I have my orders,
There will be no stowaways. No gatecrashers
At my party. A party starting soon.

And the sooner the better. Like a grounded
Astronaut I grow daily more impatient.
Am on tenterhooks. Each night
I ask the Lord to get on with it.
I fear sometimes He has forsaken us,
We His favourite children. Meek, drilled,
And ready to inherit an earth, newly-cleansed.

I scan the headlines, watch the screen.
A doctor thrilling at each fresh tumour:
The latest invasion, a breakdown of talks.
I pray for malignancy. The self-induced
Sickness for which there is only one cure:
Radium treatment. The final absolution.
That part of full circle we have yet to come.

Icarus Allsorts

'A meteorite is reported to have landed
in New England. No damage is said . . .'

A littlebit of heaven fell
From out the sky one day
It landed in the ocean
Not so very far away
The General at the radar screen
Rubbed his hands with glee
And grinning pressed the button
That started World War Three.

From every corner of the earth
Bombs began to fly
There were even missile jams
No traffic lights in the sky
In the times it takes to blow your nose
The people fell, the mushrooms rose

'House!' cried the fatlady
As the bingohall moved to various parts
of the town

'Raus!' cried the German butcher
as his shop came tumbling down

Philip was in the countinghouse
Counting out his money
The Queen was in the parlour
Eating bread and honey
When through the window
Flew a bomb
And made them go all funny

In the time it takes to draw a breath
Or eat a toadstool, instant death

The rich
Huddled outside the doors of their fallout shelters
Like drunken carolsingers

The poor
Clutching shattered televisions
And last week's editions of *T.V. Times*
(but the very last)

Civil defence volunteers
With their tin hats in one hand
And their heads in the other

C.N.D. supporters
Their ban the bomb badges beginning to rust
Have scrawled 'I told you so' in the dust.

A littlebit of heaven fell
From out the sky one day
It landed in Vermont
North-Eastern U.S.A.
The general at the radar screen
He should have got the sack
But that wouldn't bring
Three thousand million, seven hundred,
    and sixty-eight people back,
Would it?

Three Rusty Nails

Mother, there's a strange man
Waiting at the door
With a familiar sort of face
You feel you've seen before.

Says his name is Jesus
Can we spare a couple of bob
Says he's been made redundant
And now can't find a job.

Yes I think he is a foreigner
Egyptian or a Jew
Oh aye, and that reminds me
He'd like some water too.

Well shall I give him what he wants
Or send him on his way?
OK I'll give him 5p
Say that's all we've got today.

And I'll forget about the water
I suppose it's a bit unfair
But honest, he's filthy dirty
All beard and straggly hair.

*   *   *

Mother, he asked about the water
I said the tank had burst
Anyway I gave him the coppers
That seemed to quench his thirst.

He said it was little things like that
That kept him on the rails
Then he gave me his autographed picture
And these three rusty nails.

Mother the Wardrobe is Full of Infantrymen

mother the wardrobe is full of infantrymen
i did i asked them
but they snarled saying it was a mans life

mother there is a centurion tank in the parlour
i did i asked the officer
but he laughed saying 'Queens regulations'
(piano was out of tune anyway)

mother polish your identity bracelet
there is a mushroom cloud in the backgarden
i did i tried to bring in the cat
but it simply came to pieces in my hand
i did i tried to whitewash the windows
but there weren't any
i did i tried to hide under the stairs
but i couldn't get in for civil defence leaders
i did i tried ringing candid camera
but they crossed their hearts

i went for a policeman but they were looting the town
i went out for a fire engine but they were all upside down
i went for a priest but they were all on their knees
mother don't just lie there say something please
mother don't just lie there say something please

At Lunchtime

When the bus stopped suddenly
to avoid damaging
a mother and child in the road,
the younglady in the green hat sitting opposite,
was thrown across me,
and not being one to miss an opportunity
i started to make love.

At first, she resisted,
saying that it was too early in the morning,
and too soon after breakfast,
and anyway, she found me repulsive.
But when i explained
that this being a nuclearage
the world was going to end at lunchtime,
she took off her green hat,
put her busticket into her pocket
and joined in the exercise.

The buspeople,
and there were many of them,
were shockedandsurprised,
and amusedandannoyed.
But when word got around
that the world was going to end at lunchtime,
they put their pride in their pockets
with their bustickets
and made love one with the other.
And even the busconductor,
feeling left out,
climbed into the cab,
and struck up some sort of relationship with the driver.

That night, on the bus coming home,
we were all a little embarrassed,
especially me and the younglady in the green hat,

and we all started to say
in different ways
how hasty and foolish we had been.
But then, always having been a bitofalad,
i stood up and said it was a pity
that the world didnt nearly end every lunchtime,
and that we could always pretend.
And then it happened . . .

Quick asa crash
we all changed partners,
and soon the bus was aquiver
with white, mothball bodies doing naughty things.

And the next day
And everyday
In everybus
In everystreet
In everytown
In everycountry

People pretended
that the world was coming to an end at lunchtime.
It still hasnt.
Although in a way it has.

On Having a First Book of Poetry Published
(The day the world ended.)

Oh, what dreadful timing! It couldn't have been worse!
For that long-awaited, ground-breaking volume of verse.

A title to die for, an immaculate cover,
Cool photo on the back, then Bang it's all over.

Your publisher hired a publicist to titillate the press
(a review already promised in the *TLS*, no less).

Fingers crossed for Waterstones and a window display
The launch in Covent Garden, and the following day

a signing at Harrods (you've dreamed of this for yonks)
Practising your signature, you wore out two Mont Blancs.

Then the poetry-reading circuit (50 mins, plus Q & A)
Dropping by at bookstores and libraries on the way.

A choice of Literary Festivals (Cheltenham, Hay-on-Wye)
Chats on local radio, and perhaps one day on Sky.

But, oh, what lousy timing, how could anybody guess
Your career as a poet would last an hour or less.

Yes, it would have been marvellous, it would have been splendid
If you hadn't had it published on the day the world ended.

Let me Die a Youngman's Death

Let me die a youngman's death
not a clean & inbetween
the sheets holywater death
not a famous-last-words
peaceful out of breath death

When I'm 73
& in constant good tumour
may I be mown down at dawn
by a bright red sports car
on my way home
from an allnight party

Or when I'm 91
with silver hair
& sitting in a barber's chair
may rival gangsters
with hamfisted tommyguns burst in
& give me a short back & insides

Or when I'm 104
& banned from the Cavern
may my mistress
catching me in bed with her daughter
& fearing for her son
cut me up into little pieces
& throw away every piece but one

Let me die a youngman's death
not a free from sin tiptoe in
candle wax & waning death
not a curtains drawn by angels borne
'what a nice way to go' death

Summer with Monika

they say the sun shone now and again
but it was generally cloudy
with far too much rain

they say babies were born
married couples made love
(often with eachother)
and people died
(sometimes violently)

they say it was an average
                        ordinary
                        moderate
                        run of the mill
                        commonorgarden
                        summer
. . . but it wasn't

for i locked a yellowdoor
and i threw away the key
and i spent summer with monika
and monika spent summer with me

unlike everybody else
we made friends with the weather . . .
mostdays the sun called
                        and sprawled
allover the place
or the wind blew in
as breezily as ever
and ran its fingers through our hair
but usually
it was the moon that kept us company

somedays we thought about the seaside
and built sandcastles on the blankets
and paddled in the pillows
or swam in the sink
and played with the shoals of dishes

otherdays we went for long walks
around the table
and picnicked on the banks
of the settee
or just sunbathed lazily
in front of the fire
until the shilling set on the horizon

we danced a lot that summer . . .
bosanovaed by the bookcase
or maddisoned instead
hulligullied by the oven
or twisted round the bed

at first we kept birds
in a transistor box
to sing for us
but sadly they died
we being too embraced in eachother
to feed them

but it didn't really matter
because we made lovesongs with our bodies
i became the words
and she put me to music

they say it was just
                    like
                    anyother
                    summer

            . . . but it wasn't

for we had love and eachother
and the moon for company
when i spent summer with monika
and
>   monika
>   spent summer
>   withme

2

ten milk bottles standing in the hall
ten milk bottles up against the wall
next door neighbour thinks we're dead
hasnt heard a sound he said
doesnt know weve been in bed
the ten whole days since we were wed

noone knows and noone sees
we lovers doing as we please
but people stop and point at these
ten milk bottles a-turning into cheese

ten milk bottles standing day and night
ten different thicknesses and
different shades of white
persistent carolsingers without a note to utter
silent carolsingers a-turning into butter

now she's run out of passion
and theres not much left in me
so maybe we'll get up
and make a cup of tea
then people can stop wondering
what they're waiting for
those ten milk bottles a-queuing at our door
those ten milk bottles a-queuing at our door

3

saturday morning
time for stretching
and yawning
the languid
heavy lidded
lovemaking
the smile
the kiss
the 'who do you love?'
and then the weekly
confidence trick:
the yoursaying its my
turn to make the tea
and the my getting out
of bed and making it

4

our love will be an epic film
with dancing songs and laughter
the kind in which the lovers meet
and live happy everafter

our love will be a famous play
with lots of bedroom scenes
you are twenty-two you are monika
and only we know what that means

5

when the moon is waiting
for the first bus home
and birds assemble
for morning prayers
in the ticktock blanketness
of our dunlopillolove

you open your secret door
and i tiptoe in
quietly
for fear of waking the alarmclock

6

you give me the eye i sigh
and feign disinterest
you pretend to cry
and put me to the test
(a cunning little ruse)
i think 'ha ha',
you wink and far
be it from me to refuse

how you love it
when youre being teased
the eye that weeps most
when best pleased

7

take ahold of my mind
and gently but firmly
push it between your thighs
and in that warm numbness
let it remain
whilst you go about the house
doing your sweet everyday things

8

thistime
let there be no goodbyes
letsstillbefriends
parting is such
sicklysweet sorrow

let us holdhands
and think not of tomorrow
but of our dailyselves

for there's love here
such love
as makes unhappiness
appear to have mislaid our address

9

i have lately learned to swim
and now feel more at home
in the ebb and flow of your slim
rhythmic tide
than in the fullydressed
          couldntcareless
restless world outside

10

monika
i love you more
than all my redleather waistcoats
and i will never give you away
to the nastyman
who lives at the end of the road

11

if i were a parkkeeper
i would strollacross the summerlawns
of your mind
and with a pointedstick
collect all the memories
which lie about
like empty cigarettepackets

and in a distantcorner
where you could not see
i would burn them in the shade
of your love for me

12

you squeeze my hand and
   cry alittle
you cannot comprehend the
   raggletaggle of living
and think it unfair that
   Death
should be the only one
who knows what he's doing

13

you're afraid of the BIG BAD DARK
which loiters in our room
the night it prowls about the yard
the wind howls in distress
a peepingtom moon at the window
waits for the table to undress

it'll soon be tomorrow
there's nothing to fear
you whisper 'never leave me'
then
     put your
        tongue
           in my ear

14

sometimes at dawn you awake
and naked creep across our orangeroom
and drawing aside
our prettyyellowcurtains

gaze at the neatroofed horizon
of our littletown
waiting for the sun
screaming with dull pain
to rise like a spark
from a crematorium chimney
then you pitterpad back to bed
your head aflame with fear
you lie in my arms
and you lie:
'i'm happy here
so happy here'

15

KNOCK KNOCK
shhhhh . . .
dont open it
it can only be . . .

                    the ENEMY!!

16

It's got to be done
to be done right away
monika dont argue
do as i say

i've put out the milkman
and wound up the maid
its well after midnight
so dont be afraid

yes leave the light on
theres so much to see
now monika fetch the razorblade
and lie next to me

17

you are so very beautiful
i cannot help admiring
your eyes so often sadnessful
and lips so kissinspiring

i think about my being-in-love
and touch the flesh you wear so well
i think about my being-in-love
and wish you were as well
                         as well
and wish you were as well

18

i often have the feeling
that when tidying the flat
you are not thinking
of shoes, newspapers
and trivia like that
but of a skullwhite building
where all the inmates
talk poetry to scrambled eggs
and whistle at operatingtable legs
a home for Incurable Romantics
a place to end my days
you will surely have me committed
i must rise and mend my ways

19

away from you
i feel a great emptiness
a gnawing loneliness

with you
i get that reassuring feeling
of wanting to escape

20

you dont say anything
but your eyes tell me
that my standing naked
to seduce the moon
and my crying because
she walked right past
is sadly symptomatic
of a fatal attack of
'push your icy fingers
into my brain
its so hot and lonely here'

21

when the hadtohappen time came
and you quit our hadbeenhappy bed
you pulled the blankets o'er my head
and left me on my sadandlonely own

now i listen darkly to the memory of your smell
and wonder when the sun will melt the storm
our love is like a kitten in a well
the death of something young and softlywarm
the death of something of uncertainform

22

last sundaymorning
when holypictures
fluttered
on dusty church floors
when dockers snored
and mams went heavy
on the gravy browning
you got out of bed
and picking up a hatchet
whose name was

'iloveyoubutwecantgo
onlikethis'
you murdered me
brutifully
then with my tears
still singing
on your hands
you went to your mothers
for telly and a liedown

23

you are a woman of many faces
and the one that suits you best
i fear
is the one you wear when i'm not here
for when you wear your marriage face
boredom lounges round the place

24

you should never have said that
now
your smiles are whiteelephants
and your face a photograph
to be come across
some slow brown sunday

you should never have said that
your tongue is a mother without pity
now
love is gone
andanonymous
like the death of a bird in a city

25

we endure cold days and nights
    out on the moors
though we dont like the
    countryside at all

but by spending all our time
    out of doors
we dont have to see the
    writing on the wall

26

monika your soups getting cold
its cream of chicken too
why are you looking at me like that
why have your lips turned blue?

we simply cant go on like this
fighting tooth and nail
why are you looking at me like that
why has your face grown pale?

youre enough to drive a man insane
go completely off his head
why are you looking at me like that
why has your dress gone red?

the only thing i'm sorry about
is that we came to blows
why are you looking at me like that
have i got crumbs on my nose?

alright, i'm sorry i hit you so hard
but nexttime do as youre told
why are you looking at me like that
monika your soups getting cold

27

your finger
sadly
has a familiar ring
about it

28

where have the sunshine breakfasts gone?
orange juice and bacon
the morning kiss and toothpastesmile
you seem to have forsaken

now its greasy grimaces
eggs fried stormyside up
burnt threats and curdled anger
tears in a dirty cup

29

you have gone
you say forever,
and i hear nothing
but the clatter of old leaves on stone floors

30

the sky has nothing to say
and the scaffoldings are full of dead birds
the moon has passed away
and the wind has tears in its eyes
now even the policemen have gone home
and scattered like memories old and worn
the litter
        has
            inherited
                the dawn

31

sitting alone
with my bottle of sauce
KNOCK KNOCK
'who's there?'
noone of course

32

once upon a love
we spent our nights
blowing kisses across
the pillow
now we spend them
throwing plates across the kitchen

33

don't think i'm moaning
or trying to protest
but do you really need
another new dress?
why not smile
its cheaper and just as pretty

34

. . . and when Death comes in
with his zip undone
you'll give in
as you've always done . . .

35

lastnight
was your night out
and just before you went
you put your SCOWLS
in a tumbler
half filled with steradent

(so that they'd keep nice and fresh for me)

36

said i trusted you
spoke too soon
heard of your affair
with the maninthemoon
say its allover
then if you're right
why does he call
at the house everynight?

37

i have a war on my hands
each night i lie awake
and snipe at terrorists
who run naked
through the steaming jungles
of your dreams
i am on your side
but you dont care
you are asleep and unaware
of my futile heroics
my fear is that one night
i might fall asleep
and you will be captured
my sorrow is that you probably wouldn't mind
(why else keep a white flag under the pillow?)

38

once i paid the piper
and called the tune
but one afternoon
returning home
earlier than usual
i found you in bed
with the piper

you called the last waltz
and now i dance sadly
out of your life

1-2-3

1-2-3

1-2-3

39

i wanted
my castle in the air
but it vanished
without trace

i wanted
my pie in the sky
but you gave it me
in the face

40

monika who's been eating my porridge
while i've been away
my quaker oats are nearly gone
what have you got to say?

someone's been at my whisky
taken the jaguar keys
and monika, another thing
whose trousers are these?

i love and trust you darling
can't really believe you'd flirt
but there's a strange man under the table
wearing only a shirt

there's someone in the bathroom
someone behind the door
the house is full of naked men
monika! don't you love ME anymore?

41

monika the teathings are taking over!
the cups are as big as bubblecars
they throttle round the room
tinopeners skate on the greasy plates
by the light of the silvery moon
the biscuits are having a party
they're necking in our breadbin
thats jazz you hear from the saltcellars
but they don't let nonmembers in
the eggspoons had our eggs for breakfast
the saucebottle's asleep in our bed
i overheard the knives and forks
'it won't be long' they said
'it won't be long' they said.

it all started yesterday evening
as i was helping the potatoes
off with their jackets
i heard you making a date
with the kettle
i distinctly
heard you making a date
with the kettle
my kettle

then at midnight
in the halflight
while i was polishing the bluespeckles
in a famous soappowder
i saw you fondling
the fryingpan
i distinctly
saw you fondling the frying
my frying pan

finally at middawn
in the halfnight
while waiting in the coolshadows
beneath the sink
i saw you makinglove
with the gascooker
i distinctly
saw you makinglove
with the gascooker
my gascooker

my mistake was to leapupon you crying
'MONIKA THINK OF THE SAUCERS!'
for now i'm alone
you having left me for someone
with a bigger kitchen

43

in october
when winter the lodger the sod
came a-knocking at our door
i set in a store
of biscuits and whisky
you filled the hotwaterbottle with tears
and we went to bed until spring

in april
we arose
warm and smelling of morning
we kissed the sleep from eachothers eyes
and went out into the world

and now summer's here again
regular as the rentman
but our lives are now more ordered more arranged
the kissing wildly carefree times have changed

we nolonger stroll along the beaches of the bed
or snuggle in the longgrass of the carpets
the room nolonger a world for makebelieving in
but a ceiling and four walls that are for living in

we nolonger eat our dinner holding hands
or neck in the backstalls of the television
the room nolonger a place for hideandseeking in
but a container that we use for eatandsleeping in

our love has become
                    as comfortable
as the jeans you lounge about in
as my old green coat

                    as necessary
as the change you get from the milkman
for a five pound note

our love has become
                          as nice
as a cup of tea in bed
                    as simple
as something the baby said

monika
          the sky is blue
          the leaves are green
          the birds are singing
          the bells are ringing
          for me and my gal
          the suns as big as an icecream factory
          and the corn is as high as an elephant's
i could go on for hours about the beautiful
weather we're having but monika
          they dont
          make summers
          like they
          used to . . .

Summer with the Monarch

The Queen came up to Liverpool
   To dine at our Town Hall
In the evening wrote to her husband
   'Dear Philip, I'm having a ball

I think I'll hang around
   I mean everything's happening here
I'm beginning to dig the poetry scene
   And the ale, as they say, is the gear.'

So while she was having a castle built
   Down in Castle Street
She had a look round Liverpool 8
   Found a pad there, small but neat

She moved in a few belongings
   Corgis, crown, a throne
And blueblood in the neighbourhood
   Really raised the tone

Soon Her Majesty was caught up
   In the bohemian social whirl
Our gracious teenybopper
   Everybody's girl

I met her at a party
   Somewhere in Norris Green
I was just a layabout
   And she was queen of the scene

But love knows no class barriers
   As you well rightly know
And as I'd had a few that night
   I thought I'd have a go

We had a couple of dances
   As a matter of fact we raved
And when I asked 'Can I take you home?'
   She simply smiled and waved

And she told me next morning
   'I'll never love another
I've always fancied weirdos
   I appoint you Royal Lover.'

The same day we decided
   To set the social pace
And once we'd laced our sneakers
   There was noone in the race

We'd go everynight to the alehouse
   Throw down a few black 'n' tans
She'd roll a joint in the Ladies
   And we'd crawl back home on our hands

Our world was mad and frenzied
   The sun refused to set
Our joy seemed neverending
   A life of fun – and yet

Happiness is mis-shaped
   As I was soon to learn
For now this little story
   Takes on a sadder turn

For the Establishment was angry
   And to everyone's surprise
Her husband and the Prime Minister
   Were planning her demise

They kidnapped her one morning
   While I was still in bed
Took her to the Tower
   And chopped off her head

now sadly i remember
with tears for company
how i spent summer with the monarch
and
     the monarch
          spent summer
             with me.

happiness

lying in bed ofa weekdaymorning
Autumn
and the trees
none the worse for it.
Youve just got up
to make tea toast and a bottle
leaving pastures warm
for me to stretch into

in his cot
the littlefella
outsings the birds

Plenty of honey in the cupboard.
Nice.

Buddies

We were drafted into the same unit
and shipped out to the front
Shared the same lousy rations
became buddies all through the war
Two guns are better than one
that's what buddies are for

We fought the enemy side by side
and occasionally fought eachother
When they gave us hell
we gave them more
Cried after the first battle
that's what buddies are for

Then peace broke out
and we sailed into the orangeblossom sunset
Wondered how long it would last
once we were safe ashore
Now you tell me we're having our first baby
that's what buddies are for

un

the baby
fourteen months
to the month
moans in the heat
of a summer, come late
with a vengeance.

2 a.m.
and allover the city
bodies sweat
and tingle, the wearers
dancing, wending home,
or fast un asleep.

Amateur traumatics

When you starred in *my* play
you were just right.
I gave you rave notices
night after night.

But you wanted bigger and better parts.
Upstarts
sent you script after script.
You counted your lines
then you flipped. You just flipped.

bravado

and you still havent ironed
the trousers of my s.s. uni
form. The baby you say
will grow to love a new
father. Someone will come
and do my job properly.
Someone not closed.

beneath the sheets
i pick my nails
and flick
dirtpellets
soundlessly
into the darkness.
Bravado.

Vandal

at first
we had a landscape to ourselves
Then the vandals moved in

deflowered the verges
put the carp before the horse
             and worse
chopped down our initialled trees
bonfired the bench
on which we'd had our first kiss
threw stones
and chased you away

This morning
one of them was caught
He turned out to be me
I am due to appear in court next week
Charged
with emotion

Bulletins

We sit in front of the wireless
waiting for the latest news
on the state of our affair
You knitting socks for our footballers overseas
me wishing i was there
The bulletins are more frequent now
they are broadcast by the hour
The headline in the *Echo* reads
'Love turned Sour'

Trenchwarfare

after the battle of the Incriminating Loveletter
there came an uneasy truce
We still sleep together in the same trench
but you have built
a wall of sandbags in between

somenights
gutsy and fulloffight
rifle in hand
I'm over the top
brave asa ram

and you're always waiting,
my naked sentry
'Halt, who goes there? Friend or lover?'
'Lover'
'Advance lover'

in the morning
whistling 'itsalongwaytotipperary'
i trudge across the duckboards
to the bathroom

McGough's last stand

First Reel

it can't just end like this
no one to witness my plight
no sense of history
not a photographer in sight

broken promises lie thick on the ground
and i'm down to my last keg of nostalgia

tears running down your warpaint
you close in
screaming:
'white man make love with forked tongue!'

Hurrah! here comes the cavalry

End of First Reel

Second Reel

Oh no!
it's a platoon of exlovers
led by your first husband
(saturday morning matinees were never like this)
it's all over
the Battle of Shit Creek

At sundown
on an upturned wagon
a lone bugler plays the Last Post
i ask you for a dance
you give me a belt
to my scalp

THE END

Cake

i wanted one life
you wanted another
we couldn't have our cake
so we ate eachother.

tigerdreams

i go to sleep on all fours
ready to pounce
on any dream
in which you might appear
Claws withdrawn
i want you live
the image fresh as meat
i want you live
the memories flesh to eat
Every nightmare it's the same
prowling through forests
growling your name
until the alarmclock cracks the first twig
and lifting the blankets
i collapse
into the undergrowth

tightrope

at 7.55 this morning
the circus ran away to join me

there is a lion in the wardrobe
and in the pantry
the clown
goes
    down
        on the bareback rider

the seal in the bath is wearing my hat
and the elephants
have shat on the cat on the mat

my wife (always a dwarf at heart)
juggles naked for the ringmaster
who lashes her approvingly

i stagger out of bed
to shew the tightropewalkers
a thing or two.

Hash Wednesday

last wednesday
it all clicked

you only wanted me for my loveandaffection
my generosity
and my undyingfaithfulness

(to you my prizegiven rosaries meant nothing,
my holy relics, merely relics)

Begone oh Belial's daughter
I wash my hands of you in holy water

next year i will live alone
and brēed racehorses
in the attic

The Mongrel

When i came to live with you
i brought a brighteyed pup
and as our love matured
so the pup grew up

you fed him and you trained him
asif he were your own
you pampered him looked after him
until he was full grown

then you went away
    now he's uncontrollable
                inconsolable

mistresses they come and go
look pretty much the same
they pat his head and stroke his back
and say they're glad they came

but he's no longer interested
in feminine acclaim
and when they try new tricks
he tires quickly of the game

he skulks around the kitchen
looking old and slightly lame
at night he howls at the window
asif the moon's to blame

and with every sad encounter
i realize to my shame
that my sadeyed mongrel
answers only to your name.

10 *Ways to Make a Killing on the Stock Market*

1 Get out of bed early and frequently.
  Remember, punctuality is the investor's best friend.
2 Resist the temptation to dress too gaudily.
3 Keep your figures neat and your columns orderly.
4 Avoid fatty foods.
5 Whatever you do . . . Whichever way we . . . I mean.
6 Your face. I think of your face. Your body.
7 Enfranchise non-voting 'A' shares through a rights issue.

8 Pain. The tears. But the laughter. We must never forget the
   laughter.
9 Not too late. Don't leave me. Please don't leave . . .
10

All Over bar the Shouting

It's all over.
Almost a bar-room brawl.

Shouting does not become you.
Becomes you not at all.

It becomes me.
Shouting becomes me.

I become shouting.
I shout and shout and shout.

I shout until shouting
and I are one.

You walk out.
Leave me lock-

jawed in shout.
Dumbstuck.

Into the bar
the ghosts of years come streaming.

It's all over,
bar the shouting. Bar the screaming.

The Perfect Crime

The sword-swallower
stabbed his unfaithful
wife to death

Before disposing
of the murder weapon
in one gulp.

Last Lullaby

The wind is howling,
    My handsome, my darling,
An illwisher loiters
    Outside in the street.
The pain in your breastbone
    Tightens and tightens
And you are alone,
    My treasure, my sweet.

Gone is your lover,
    My angel, my dearest,
Gone to another
    To hold and caress.
Could that shadow you see
    On the curtain be me?
Of course not, beloved,
    Goodnight and God bless.

Are they not gentle,
    My naughty, my precious,
These hands that will bring you
    To sleep by and by?
Sweet dreams, my sweetheart,
    Hush, don't you cry.
Daddy will sing you
    A last lullaby.

Daddy will sing you
    A last lullaby.

You and I

I explain quietly. You
hear me shouting. You
try a new tack. I
feel old wounds reopen.

You see both sides. I
see your blinkers. I
am placatory. You
sense a new selfishness.

I am a dove. You
recognize the hawk. You
offer an olive branch. I
feel the thorns.

You bleed. I
see crocodile tears. I
withdraw. You
reel from the impact.

40 — Love

middle	aged
couple	playing
ten	nis
when	the
game	ends
and	they
go	home
the	net
will	still
be	be
tween	them

No Message

At first, picture postcards
Next to my address:
A blank stare

The occasional letter
Envelope torn open to reveal:
An empty page

The late-night phone call
I recognize the intake of your breath
But no voice

Finally, the bottle
Washed up on the beach
by the morning tide

Pulling out the cork
I remove the slip of paper
In your handwriting it says:

'No Message.'

A golden life

We live a simple life
my wife and I. Are
the envy of our friends.
We are artists. Skilled craftsmen.
I am good with my hands
She with hers.
I am a goldsmith
She a masseuse.

I design and make
gold lockets that cannot be opened
necklaces that will not fasten
ornate keys for which there are no locks.

Trinkets to buy and hoard
toys for the rich and bored.
Things useless, but beautiful.

Compared with the objects I make,
I am dull.
My wife is not dull,
She is exciting.
After a hard day at the parlour
or visiting hotels
(I do not pry)
She comes home
tired, but exciting.

I give her something golden
each evening something new.
It makes her smile.
She rewards me with her golden body
which I melt and shape at will.
Fashioning, with consummate skill,
the precious metal of her flesh.

We live a golden life
my wife and I. Dream
golden dreams. And
each golden morning
go our golden ways.
Make golden dreams for strangers.
Golden nights
and golden days.

P.O.W.

it wouldn't be wise to go away together
not even for a weekend.
A few bouts of neocopulation
in a Trust House in the Midlands
would not be the answer.

I commit my sins gentle
Prefer my adultery mental.

Though we feel the need to escape
sometimes
The need for a scape-
goat sometimes
You my muddled tunnel
I your Wooden Horse
We'd only keep running all night
then give ourselves up at first light.

You see I don't love you
And though you're as beautiful as she was
it wouldn't be wise to go away together.
My sense of duty would trouble you
I'm a semi-detached P.O.W.

Three weeks ago we decided to go our separate ways

Three weeks ago we decided to go our separate ways
not overnight, but whenever was convenient.

There is a fragility now
about our lovemaking
asif each time might be the last
The finger tends to linger
where once it hurried past.

And as the end of our relationship looms
the excitement of the start it assumes.
There are new awakenings
erotic as in a dream
With each sacrificial offering
the more virginal we seem
Old scars become new wounds
when kissed overmuch
And memories longhardened
now moisten to the touch.

Love is a circle
we've completed the course
Now we savour the honeymoon
before the divorce.

And with all we've discovered together
And with all the experience gained
that final
mad
sad
fuck
will achieve the perfection
that only the first attained
That final
mad
sad

The Rot

Some years ago the Rot set in.
It began in a corner of the bedroom
following the birth of the second child.
It spread into the linen cupboard
and across the fabric of our lives.
Experts came to treat it.
Could not.
The Rot could not be stopped.

Dying now, we live with it.
The fungus grows.
It spreads across our faces.
We watch the smiles rot,
gestures crumble.
Diseased, we become the disease.
Part of the fungus.
The part that dreams. That feels pain.

We are condemned.
Things dying, that flaunt their dying,
that cannot hide, are demolished.
We will rot eachother no longer.
From the street outside
comes the sound of the drill,
as men, hungry for dust,
close in for the kill.

Head Injury

I do not smile because I am happy.
Because I gurgle I am not content.
I feel in colours, mottled, mainly black.
And the only sound I hear is the sea
Pounding against the white cliffs of my skull.

For seven months I lay in a coma.
Agony.
Darkness.
My screams drowned by the wind
Of my imperceptible breathing.

One morning the wind died down. I awoke.

You are with me now as you are everyday
Seeking some glimmer of recognition
Some sign of recovery. You take my hand.
I try to say: 'I love you.'
Instead I squawk,
Eyes bobbing like dead birds in a watertank.
I try to say: 'Have pity on me, pity on yourself
Put a bullet between the birds.'
Instead I gurgle.
You kiss me then walk out of the room.
I see your back.
I feel a colour coming, mottled, mainly black.

Mouth

I went to the mirror
but the mirror was bare,
looked for my mouth
but my mouth wasn't there.
Over the lips had grown
a whiskered hymen of skin.

I went to the window
wanting to shout
I pictured the words
but nothing came out.
The face beneath the nose
an empty hoarding.

And as I waited, I could feel
flesh filling in the space behind.
Teeth melted away tasting of snow
as the stalactites of the palate
joined the stalagmites below.
The tongue, like a salted snail,
sweated and shrivelled.

The doctor has suggested plastic surgery:
a neat incision, cosmetic dentistry
and full red lips (factory fresh).
He meant well but I declined.

After all, there are advantages.
At last I have given up smoking,
and though food is a needle
twice a day, it needs no cooking.
There is little that I miss.
I never could whistle and there's no one to kiss.

In the street, people pass by
unconcerned. I give no one directions
and in return am given none.
When asked if I am happy
I look the inquisitor straight in the eye
and think to myself . . . ("

Holiday on Death Row

1

new dead flowers in
living room. First
Wasp of Spring. Time
for writing. Sap and
dying. Ashes and seed
lie scattered etc.
In kitchen, Wife
cook sunday dinner
for herself. Upstairs
Husband push drawing
pins into scowling
mouth of penis.

2

Wife is out. Has taken
clichés to launderette.
Husband, withdrawn, stare
overlong at photographs
of himself, in hope
of being recognised.
In front of mirrors
he bob and weave,
turn suddenly to catch
reflection off guard.
Reflection always on time.
On occasions, lying in wait.

3

Wife, downstairs midnight
putting cholesterol in his
Flora, decide their life
together has become anathema.
Stuffed toad in birdcage.
Husband, upstairs writing
poems she will never
read, decide holiday
abroad would be best
thing for both of them.
Next day he leave for Anathema.
Wife give toad kiss of life.

4

Husband, penis loaded
with drawing pins, swagger
into kitchen. Unimpressed,
Wife snarl matteroffactly.
'You rat a tat tat
        rat a tat tat
Take that a tat tat.'
Wife is pinned against wall
like fading Wanted Poster.
Husband pack away
empty shotgun and return
upstairs to collect reward.

5

she hang on his every word.
Pull, pull and pull.
Hand to his mouth
he fight back. Wife
drag him to floor.
Words cry out in pain:
'Words, we're only words,
we don't mean anything.'
Wife release grip
and return to kitchen.
'That what you always
say.' She say.

6

in Husband's dreams, her
stockings burst at seams.
She is centre-fold
of all his magazines.
Pinned up each night,
she disport herself
as he befit. As he
thought she used to do
or might have done.
Prickteasing series of
saucy pix. His memory
playing safe, playing tricks.

7

except for sound of their breathing.
In bed Husband mustn't touch.
Put arms around body he
helped shape. He fight impulse.
Do what is not natural.
Keep his self to himself.
Nerve ends tingle. He become
Electric Chair and move in.
She asleep on Death Row.
He wonder what would be
her last request. Chair
get erection. Chair know best.

8

Wife hoard hazelnuts
in cunt Husband
train squirrels to
fetch hazelnuts. Wife
keep fox in petticoats
to chase squirrels. At
break of day, Husband,
in coat so gay, unleash
hounds in bedroom to catch
fox. Wife join Anti-blood-
sports League. Husband join
Anti-nuts-in-cunts Brigade.

9

Wife want life of own.
Husband want life of Wife.
Husband hire hitman.
Hitman hit Wife.
Wife hit back.
Hit, hitman run.
Wife run harder.
Hurt hitman.
Hurt hitman hit Husband.
Tired Husband hire second
hitman to fire first hitman.
Fired hitman retire, hurt.

10

Husband keep live rat down
front of jeans for rainy day.
One rainy day, drunk on
cooking sherry, Wife slip
hand inside Husband's jeans.
With brutal strokes she
skin it alive before
pulling off its head.
Wiping blood on pinny
she return to cakemix.
Husband bury dead rat
for another year.

11

upstairs, Husband wrestle
with major themes. Wife
in kitchen putting
two and two together.
Always Wife in kitchen.
Always Husband wrestling.
On kitchen table is
flour, water, drawing pins,
salt, blood, ashes etc.
On desk upstairs,
major themes (or parts
thereof) lie scattered etc.

12

photographs of hitmen.
Hazelnuts for rainy day.
Dead flowers in fading
penis. Clichéd toad
bursting at seams. Empty
shotgun in birdcage. Holiday
on Death Row. Words,
we're only words.
Husband, upstairs, painting
out light in painting
of end of tunnel. Wife
in garden, digging up rat.

Goodbat Nightman

God bless all policemen
and fighters of crime,
May thieves go to jail
for a very long time.

They've had a hard day
helping clean up the town,
Now they hang from the mantelpiece
both upside down.

A glass of warm blood
and then straight up the stairs,
Batman and Robin
are saying their prayers.

*   *   *

They've locked all the doors
and they've put out the bat,
Put on their batjamas
(They like doing that)

They've filled their batwater-bottles
made their batbeds,
With two springy battresses
for sleepy batheads.

They're closing red eyes
and they're counting black sheep,
Batman and Robin
are falling asleep.

P.C. Plod at the Pillar Box

It's snowing out
streets are thiefproof
A wind that blows
straight up yer nose
no messin
A night
not fit to be seen with a dog
out in

On the corner
P.C. Plod (brave as a mountain lion)
passes the time of night
with a pillar box
'What's 7 times 8 minus 56?'
he asked mathematically
The pillar box was silent for a moment
and then said
nothing
'Right first time,'
said the snowcapped cop
and slouched off towards Bethlehem
Avenue

P.C. Plod in Love

Sergeant Lerge put down his knife and fork
and turning to Plod, said
'Yummy yum yummy, yummy yummy yum yum'
and began to lick his lips.
'Stop licking my lips' said Plod
and moved further down the table.
The sergeant apologised. 'Sorry constable,
forgot myself for a minute . . . bad habit I got into
at police college.' And muttering something

about the way the light from the canteen window
brought a magical softness to Plod's cheeks,
he stood up and flustered his way out.
Plod, his appetite gone, pushed away the remains
of his sultana pud and went into a brown study.

Five minutes later there was a knock on the study door.
'Come' said Plod. In came the lovely Policewoman Hodges.
'Sorry to disturb you constable, but I believe
I left my handbag on the chair behind you.'
Plod stood to let her pass, and as she did
he felt her serge with pleasure.
This was the moment he'd been waiting for.
'Er . . . I was wondering if . . . er . . . spare ticket for the . . . er . . .
Policeman's ball . . . er' He stumbled over the words.
W.P.C. Hodges helped him gently to his feet.
'I'd love to' she said, and without another word
(except 'Tarra, see yer Saturday') left the study,
closing the imaginary door firmly behind her.

The Sergeant gets a handsome deal

'Quiet tonight'
suggested Sergeant Lerge
seeing P.C. Plod in Boot's doorway.
'As a truncheon'
was Plod's reply (rich in simile).
'Anything at all?'
'Pair of drunks and a drug peddler Sarge.'
'Drug peddler eh. I trust you
apprehended the villain?'
'Indeed Sarge'
'What was his cargo?'
'Marijuana'
'What kind?'
'Congo red.'
'How much?'
'Twenty quid an ounce'

'Reasonable. I'll take a half'
'To you, thirty bob'
'That's a handsome deal Constable'
'You're a handsome sergeant, Sergeant.'

P.C. Plod versus the Youth International Party

P.C. Plod had just come off point duty in Yates Wine Lodge
and was making his way back to the cop shop for a meat pie
and a liedown, when he suddenly realised he was lost.
As was his custom in cases like this
he looked for a member of the public to assist him.
For purposes of this poem,
the one nearest to hand was a Yippie.
'I'm sorry to trouble you sir, but would you be so kind
as to direct me to the nearest police station?'
'Pig' said the Yippie, 'Pig.'
Plod smiled, 'Perhaps I have not made myself quite clear . . .'
The Yippie produced a water pistol from his handbag
and directed a stream into Plod's good eye.
'Pig' said the Yippie, 'Pig' 'Pig'
''pon my soul' muttered the peeved P.C.
and moving with the speed of a man twice his size
drew from beneath his policecape
a sawnoff potato shotgun. The Yippie blanched.
'Pig' he hissed. 'Badger' retorted Plod
and with deadly aim, let go four and a half rounds
of King Edwards. The youngman fell in a heap.
'Silly place to leave a heap' thought Plod
as he bareheaded to the nearest barrowlady
to refill his helmet with ammo.

On the Road

Getting on at Notting Hill
A baglady. More or less.
Big, sad and grey.
Late thirties at a guess.

Change at Euston
for the Marrakesh Express.
Elastic-band bangles,
sandal-length dress.

Layer upon layer
of embroidered tat.
Smoke-blackened mirrors,
large floppy hat.

A mucky pup
(Afghan hound?)
in hippy best.
(Morocco bound

with Crosby, Stills and Hope.)
Lamour?
Whatever happened
to l'amour?

Kohl-black eyes downcast
flutter now and then
at men who fast
avert their gaze.

Neil Young, where art thou now?
Donovan, T. Rex?
Those incensesensual days,
Sweet nights of sex.

She puffs hard her cigarette,
Lets loose the ash.
Dreams about l'amour
and Graham Nash.

Birmingham

Auschwitz with H and C
Seven a.m. and vacuum cleaners
at full throttle. Brum Brum Brum.
Grey curtains against a grey sky
Wall to wall linoleum and the
ashtray nailed to the mantelpiece.
Sacrificing breakfast for semidreams
I remember the days we stayed
at the Albany. Five Ten a night.
I was somebody then (the one on the right
with glasses singing Lily the Pink).
The Dolce Vita.

At 10 o'clock the Kommandant
(a thin spinster, prim as shrapnel)
balls me out of bed. 'Get up
or I'll fetch the police. Got guests
arriving at midday. Businessmen.
This rooms to be cleaned and ready.'
  i Kleenextissues to be uncrumpled and ironed
  ii Dust reassembled
 iii Fresh nail in the ashtray
 iv Harpic down the plughole
  v Beds to be seen and not aired.

In the lounge my fellow refugees
are cowering together for warmth.
𝕹𝖔 𝖌𝖆𝖘 𝖋𝖎𝖗𝖊𝖘 𝖆𝖑𝖑𝖔𝖜𝖊𝖉 𝖇𝖊𝖋𝖔𝖗𝖊 6.30
𝖎𝖓 𝖙𝖍𝖊 𝖊𝖛𝖊𝖓𝖎𝖓𝖌. 𝖁𝖊𝖗𝖇𝖔𝖙𝖊𝖓.
We draw straws. The loser
rings the service bell. 'Tea! Tea!!
I've got more to do than run round
making tea at all hours of the day.

Tea!!!' She goosesteps down the hall.
A strange quirk of feet.
When the bill comes there is
included a 12½% service charge.
We tell her to stick it
up her brum. La dolce vita.

Wolverhampton

spiders are holding their wintersports
in the bathroom. Skating on the
lino, skiing down the slippery
slopes of the bath. Burdened
with my British sense of fairplay
and love of animals, I shower
on tiptoe, water at half-throttle.
I try whistling a happy toon.
The walls, painted in memory
of some longdead canary have
cloth ears: grey cunard towels
folded frayed-side in. Outside
the town too is taking an
evening shower before going out
for the night. Less sensitive
than I to the creepycrawlies
creepingcrawling round its aching feet.

Bradford (i)

Saris billow in the wind like dhows off the shore
bus drivers whistle ragas above the traffic roar.
Late afternoon, and darkness already
elbowing its way through the crowded streets.
The pavements glister and are cold.
A lady, brittle with age, teeters along,

keeping balance with a shopping bag in one hand
and a giant box of cornflakes in the other.
Lovers arminarm home for hot soup and a bath-for-two.
Everyone a passer-by or a passer-through.

Up at the university, lectures are over for the day,
and students, ruddy with learning, race back to the digs
to plan revolutions to end revolutions.

When asked why he had elected to pursue mathematics
in academic seclusion, the old prof had answered:
'Because there's safety in numbers.'

Happy show.
Good to see the front row getting stoned
on a joint full of herbal tobacco
Mike hands out during his song.
And afterwards its beer out of plastic mugs
then off to the Pennyfarthing for pie and peas and dances
wi' lovely lass wi' biggest tits east of Pennines.

(ii)

Knocked up after three hours sleep
'Your seven o'clock call sir'
With Pavlovian urgency I respond and
start dressing, guilty of staying in bed,
terrified of being late, then the truth
hits me like a snowball. No call.
I hadn't ordered an early morning call.
Its a mistake, a joke, I collapse
back into bed and dream of hot pies
thundering down motorways flanked
by huge tits. Its eleven o'clock
and waking to find myself still alive
I get up and go downstairs to celebrate.
The girl at reception calls me over

'The morning papers you ordered sir'
and hands me the *Times*, *Guardian*,
Telegraph, *Express*, *Mail*, *Sun*, *Mirror*,
three copies of the *Yorkshire Post* and the *Beano*.
'I didn't order these' I quibble.
'Its written down' says she. And so it is,
in handwriting not my own. A joke.
I accept the *Beano*. On such a day
as this threatens to be who needs news.

Huddersfield

Monster cooling towers stand guard
lest the town takes to the hills,
4 p.m. and the sky the colour of frozen lard.

Secondhand soap in my little B and B.
My only comfort, the Kozeeglow hotwaterbottle,
provided free of charge after November 15.
'Could I please have a front door key?'
I ask the man on my way out.
'You won't need one' he replies,
'We don't lock up till midnight.'
I explain that being a traveller
in ladies' nighties, my work keeps me
out until the early hours. He winks
and lends me his own, personal,
oneandonly, worthitsweight in gold,
magic, back door key.

Later, having not taken Huddersfield Polytechnic
by storm, we retire to the Punjab
to lick our wounds and dangle our disappointment
in the curry. Chicken with 2 chapatis.
Home cooking. The real McCoy sahib.
Outside, no one on the tundrastreets

save we eternal action seekers.
To full to drink, too cold to laugh.
At one a.m. we give up the ghost
town and steam back to the gaff.

in bed I wear socks and my grey woolly hat,
shiver, and regret not having filled the Kozeeglow
with vindaloo.

Newcastle

All night
ghosts of ducks
longsince plucked
waddled menacingly
across the eiderdown.

in the morning
mealyeyed I stood
on the foot of the bed.
The bed yowled
and kicked me across the room.

I picked myself up
and took myself out for a walk
(unfortunately we became separated
so I had to come home alone).

Leeds

1 a.m.

alone
and the ale
wearing off
so quiet
i can hear
the eggs
shufffling

2 a.m.

i don't miss
my teddybear
only you

two hands
where its hot
in a bed
made for two

7 a.m.

alarmclock
sends fireengines
clanging into
my dreams

bedroom is cold

i reach out
and put on
my hangover

8 a.m.

rain crackles
the flags
i pour
whiskey
over my
cornflakes

moonshine breakfast

Sheffield (i)

After knocking 'em dead at the College of Ed.
we head into town for soft lights and hard liquor.
At the Cavendish there are ladies galore
on the glass-eyed floor, where Mike, John and I
stand together, the more easily to be recognised.

And we are, but by Ginger and his mates.
Steelworkers, hard as nails and big as foothills.
'Yer supposed to be comedy, make us laugh then.'
They fire their six-shooters at our feet.
We dance, they laugh. They buy the drinks,
we laugh, and so on, and so bloody on.

At chucking-out time, the roadies, as ever,
have copped off and taken the van,
leaving Comedy to trudge home in a rain that stings.

(ii)

Sometimes I dont smell so good.
Its not that I dont care about
personal hygiene. I do. Its just that
sometimes the body catches up on me.
Like when Im out all day and
refuse to pay for a wash and
brush up at the local municipal
on lack of principle. And hiding
away in some unfamiliar un
kempt saloon I console myself
theres no such thing as *bad* breath.
All breath is good. And sweat
means the body functions as it
should. I drink my bitter.
Put a pork pie to the knife.
Far sweeter than the stink of
death, is the stink of life.

Canterbury

in the no mans land
between opening hours
2 winos
compose a pietà

one
asleep on a bench
halfbottle of richruby
warm and safe
in his richruby
winepocket

the other
keeping an eye
on the cathedral.

Cardiff 6 p.m.

No. 12 a long room built under the eaves. Tri-
angular. Like living in a giant Toblerone packet.
One-bar electric fire and the meter only takes
threepenny bits. Sore throat and a cold a comin
sure as eggs is eggs is eggs.
Somewhere between here and London
the van has broken down. No band.
No props. It's going to be a fun show
at the Barry Memorial Hall.
'Drink Brains' says the advert on a beermat.
They'd drink anything down here.
Must be the coaldust and all that
choirpractice. Outside its raining oldwomen
and walkingsticks. The pillow feels damp.
Tears of the previous paying guest.
The eskimos in the room next door
speak fluent welsh at the tops
of their voices. Not a drink to be had
T.B. or not T.B. that is the question.
Pneumonia at least. Sure as eggs
is eggs is eggs is eggs is eggs
is eggs is eggs is eggs is eggs
is eggs croeso is eggs is eggs
is eggs is eggs is eggs is eggs
is eggs is eggs is eggs is eggs

Cardiff 11 a.m.

Down first for breakfast
in the neat and nic-nac tidy
diningroom I am left to my devices.
I pick up cold steel talons
and tear into the heart of Egg
which bleeds over strips of dead
pig marinated in brine.
Grey shabby Mushrooms squeal
as they are hacked to death
slithering in their own sweat.
Like policemen to a motorway accident,
Toast arrives. The debris is mopped up.
Nothing remains of the slaughter.
John comes in with Judy.
'Mornin'
'Mornin'
'Up early then?'
'Aye'
Life goes on.

Cardiff

and Cardiffs a tart with a heart of gold.
Has been for me since the Poetry Conference
back in sixty-something. All the stars
of the silver page were there. Heroes.
To kiss the mistress of the man
you actually wrote an essay about.
To see huddled in flesh and blood
the bard you thought died in the '30s.
The lecturing, the hectoring, the theorizing,
the self-opinionizing, the factions and the jealousies.
And I took my poems to a party
and nobody asked me to read.

Except Sue, afterwards. Sue, a velveteenager.
Archangelhaired and greeneyed
freeschooled and freeloving who taught me
more about poetry than any conference.

aNd tripPING tHe luMP fanTASTic with bRIan.
Spending two hours in Woolworths
just looking. Then going to the park
and listening to flowers gossiping.
                              Then
the comedown.
(Stoned out of his head, the captain
has left the bridge. Out of control
the vessel drifts toward uncertain disaster.
Shipwrecked on an iceberg of frozen sugar.)
Watching a drunk staggering
and i am the drunk. Out of sync.
Afraid of what the trafficlights might think.
Lying in bed and becoming my own heartbeat.
The monster fingers on my thighs are my own
tapping out an urgent message only they understand.
When you fall out of love with it
the body can be a foul piece of meat.

Quartered at the Park Hotel,
well-hung and drawn from all over.
3 star accommo and all expenses paid.
Hospitality is a red rag to a writer.
Brings out the beast. The muse
is bound, gagged and locked in the closet.
Then the pillaging begins. Poetic Licentiousness.
Shoes down the lift-shaft and chambertin for breakfast.
Naked ladies in corridors and dirty songs in the lounge.
'Give me football hooligans everytime'
beefs the Night porter to the Day. 'Poets? scruffs more like,
except for that nice Mr Macbeth. Coloured too, some of them.
Whoever heard of coloured poets?'

Poem for National LSD Week

Mind, how you go!

Nottingham

Stoned and lonely in the union bar
Looking for a warm student
to fall upon. Someone gentle
and undemanding. History perhaps?
Not Maths or English.

Not English. I'm in
no mood to be laid
alongside our literary heritage
allocated my place in her
golden treasury of flesh.

Geography might do the job.
To snuggle up to
shifting continents and
ocean currents. Swap tonnage
and compare monsoons.

Even Chemistry. Someone
tangible. Flasks, bubblings
and a low flame underneath.
With someone warm like this
I'd take my chances.

Maths would find in me no questions
English Lit. no answers.

9 to 5 (or cosy biscuit)

What I wouldn't give for a nine to five.
Biscuits in the right hand drawer,
teabreaks, and typists to mentally undress.

The same faces. Somewhere to hang
your hat and shake your umbrella.
Cosy. Everything in its place.

Upgraded every few years. Hobbies.
Glass of beer at lunchtime
Pension to look forward to.

Two kids. Homeloving wife.
Bit on the side when the occasion arises
H.P. Nothing fancy. Neat semi.

*   *   *

What I wouldn't give for a nine to five.
Glass of beer in the right hand drawer
H.P. on everything at lunchtime.

The same 2 kids. Somewhere to hang
your wife and shake your bit on the side.
Teabreaks and a pension to mentally undress.

The same semifaces upgraded.
Hobbies every few years, neat typists
in wet macs when the umbrella arises.

What I wouldn't give for a cosy biscuit.

Conversation on a Train

I'm Shirley, she's Mary.
We're from Swansea
(if there was a horse there
it'd be a one-horse town
but there isn't even that).
We're going to Blackpool
Just the week. A bit late I know
But then there's the Illuminations
Isn't there? No, never been before.
Paris last year. Didn't like it.
Too expensive and nothing there really.

Toy factory, and Mary works in a shop.
Grocers. Oh it's not bad
Mind you the money's terrible.
Where are you from now?
Oh aye, diya know the Beatles then?
Liar!
And what do you do for a living?
You don't say.
Diya hear that Mary?
Well I hope you don't go home
And write a bloody poem about us.

SPORTING RELATIONS

Grandma

Grandma
(All-England Cartwheeling
Champion 1944–49)
thought romance was dead

Until she met Grandpa
(a somersaulter of note)
at a Rotary Club dance
and fell heels over head.

Fig. 1

Once wed
they backflipped
down the aisle
in breathtaking style

Then cartwheeled like clockwork
throughout the day
to spend their honeymoon
unwinding, in Morecambe Bay.

Fig. 2

Uncle Malcolm

Uncle Malcolm
put the shot
for Scotland.

When he retired
he collected shots
as a hobby.

At the time
of his death
he had nearly 200.

And in accordance
with his last wishes
they were buried with him

at St Giles Cemetery in Perth.
Uncle Mal is now at rest
somewhere near the centre of the earth.

Cousin Wystan

Train-spotting
is that a sport?

It is for Cousin Wystan
until he gets caught

Armed with a paint-box
and a quiver of brushes

Around the railsheds
after midnight he rushes

He's the Seurat of the Circle Line
the Northern's Jackson Pollock

His trainscapes are spectacular
surreal, yet melancholic

His dabs and daubs deservedly
stir the imagination

Critics applaud each masterpiece
as it rattles through the station

The National and the Tate
compete for his first retro

And Paris implores him
to immortalize the Métro

But Wystan is unmoved
by popular acclaim

And dreams, not of money,
galleries or fame

But of airports,
Heathrow, Schiphol, JFK.

Security Alert!
Wystan (plane-spotter) is on his way.

Uncle Mork

Uncle Mork
was a fell-walker.
He'd take off from York
and walk and walk

over the dales
across the moors
through the vales
blisters, sores

it hurt like hell.
He walked and walked
and never talked
just walked and walked

until he fell.

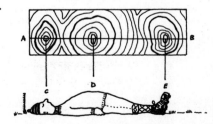

Uncle Pat

Going in to bat
against the Windies
in his first (and final) Test
Uncle Pat
wore vinyl undies
and an armour-plated vest.

But in the panic to get dressed
(wickets falling thick and fast)
left his box off.

Third ball took his rocks off.

Cousin Caroline

Cousin Caroline
was a very fine
sprinter. In the winter
of 1988, with a
bandaged knee
she ran the 100
metres in 10.3

But her best time
was in the dressing room afterwards.

Uncle Anthony

Uncle Anthony
was a low hurdler.
Being only 4' 6"
he was the lowest
hurdler in Bridlington.

In his summer of '42
he married a Northern Counties
high jumper, who,
delighted to please,
being 2 foot taller,
straddled him with ease.

Kung Fu Lee

Kung Fu Lee
a greenbelt
with a reputation second to none
was more than vexed
when annexed
and one morning built upon.

Albert Robinson

Albert Robinson
(a half-cousin by marriage)
is probably the only
bullfighter in Birmingham.

At five in the afternoon
he parades round the Bull Ring
in his Suit of Lights
(an army battledress
and panty tights
sequinned plimsolls
and padded flies)
a faraway look
in his faraway eyes.

For he struts beneath
Andalusian skies
as concrete corridors
echo the cries

of aficionados
in shoppers' disguise:
'El Robbo, El Robbo, el mas valiente matador!'

On his way to the hostel
he stops and he buys
a carton of milk
and two meat pies
then it's olé to bed
and olé to rise.

Cousin Chas

Cousin Chas,
an expert in the art
of self-defence,
would go out of his way
to defend himself.

'In an age
of senseless violence,'
he would hiss,
'there is only one language
people understand
and it's this.'

Every Saturdaynight
after a few pints
Chas and his mates
would roam the streets
looking for pale young men
against whom
they would defend themselves.

Cousin Chas
may not have been
one of Nature's gentlemen
but he was a right bastard.

Aunty Dora

A grandpiano of a woman is Aunty Dora.
Limbering up on the 60-metre board
she throws the pool into shadow.

What with the shaking and the creaking
a spectator might expect a soaking
a depthcharge of nuclear proportions

> But no.
> Her dive
> is as
> delicate
> as an
> hibiscus
> unfolding
> in slowmo.

Like thistledown on the air
she drifts, turns, almost lingers there
until her fingers tap the meniscus

The surface opens soundlessly
and pulling in her shadow after her
Aunty Dora and water are one.

Aunt Ermintrude

Aunt Ermintrude
was determined to
swim across the Channel.
Each week she'd
practise in the bath
encostumèd in flannel.

The tap end
was Cap Gris Nez
the slippy slopes
were Dover. She'd
doggypaddle up and down
vaselined all over.

After 18 months, Aunt Erm was in peak condition.
So, one cold grey morning in March
she boarded the Channel steamer at Dover
went straight to her cabin
climbed into the bath
and urged on by a few well-wishers,
Aunt Ermintrude, completely nude
swam all the way to France.
Vive la tante!

Uncle Bram

Uncle Bram
a batcatcher of distinction
scorned the use of
battraps, batnets and batpoison.
'Newfangled nonsense,'
he would scoff, and off
he would go
to hang upsidedown

in belfries
for days on end
in the hope of snatching
one of the little batstards.

Billy Our Kid

Billy our Kid
was the dandy
of the snooker halls
He affected
brocade waistcoats
of uncertain hue
and with his trusty
pearlhandled cue
hustled many an
amateur passerthrough.

In '69 he went to New Orleans
to try his luck.
Now he lives in Pittsburgh
and drives a truck.

Wild Bill Sitting Bull

Wild Bill Sitting Bull
(half cowboy, half Sioux)
confused by watching Westerns
went in search of caribou.

In the Badlands
he was strangled
by his spangled lasso

Did a wardance
then scalped himself
like a man's gotta do.

Uncle Noah

A man mountain
    was Uncle Noah
the best hammer-thrower
    in Western Samoa.

Once, in the midst
    of a magnificent throw
he lost concentration
    and forgot to let go.

Flew out of the stadium
    and up into space
a puzzled expression
    on his pustular face.

At first it was fun
    in a stomach-churning way
but once round the planet
    he called it a day.

Free of encumbrance
    the ex-hammer-thrower
plummeted earthwards
    towards Krakatoa.

Into the mouth
    of the crater he rushed
right down its throat
    like a finger, pushed.

With a gulp disappeared
    into the bubbling lava
the volcano heaved
    and threw up over Java.

Since the eruption, experts say,
    of mighty Krakatoa
Sunsets have been spectacular
    (so, thank you, Uncle Noah).

Granny

Granny plays whist
better when pwhist.

Dear Lonely Hearts

'Dear Lonely Hearts,
my name is Nate
my hobbies are weightlifting
and tempting fate.'

'Dear Nate,
my name is Kate
my hobby is weightwatching
please name the date.'

He showered her with gifts
Now Kate watches as Nate lifts.

Cousin Reggie

Cousin Reggie
who adores the sea
lives in the Midlands
unfortunately.

He surfs down escalators
in department stores
and swims in the High Street
on all of his fours.

Sunbathes on the pavement
paddles in the gutter
(I think our Reggie's
a bit of a nutter).

Angelina

Angelina
(blueblooded)
owned a yacht
and smoked pacht
a lacht.
So when things
gacht hacht
away sailed Angelina
(so regal)
to where the grass was greener
(and legal).

Uncle Sean

If they held Olympic contests
for brick-throwing
Uncle Sean would win them all
at all.

But they don't.
So he carries hods for Wimpeys
and dreams of glories
that might have been.

Uncle Sean lives in Coventry
a stone's throw away
from the Albert Hall
at all.

Merve the Swerve

Merve the Swerve
   an old tennis pro

Won the French Open
   the US and oh!

He started snorting
   lines of snow

Umpires warned
   it would end in tears

Now Mervyn's serving
   seven years.

Terry and Pancho

Last year
Terry and Pancho
won the Men's Doubles.

One had . . . uhm . . . troubles.
They were fixed.

This year
Terri and Pancho
won the Mixed.

Uncle Jack

Uncle Jack
was a very cross
country runner.
Nothing seemed
to make him happy.

With only one lung
he couldn't run fast
so he took short cuts
and still came last.

And meaner still
of Uncle Jack
some of the short cuts he took
he never gave back.

Uncle Trevor and Aunty Penny

Uncle Trevor and Aunty Penny
won the Northamptonshire
ballroom dancing championship
seven times on the foxtrot.

Practice makes perfect.
Every night after saying their prayers
they glide round the bedroom
for hours on end.

(The nightdress Aunty Penny
wears, she made herself
out of 250 yards
of floral winceyette.)

Uncle Trevor, however,
made of sterner stuff
to's and fro'ze
in the buff.

Cousin Horatio

Cousin Horatio
won a ten pound bet
by rowing across the Atlantic
singlehanded. Six months later

he confessed to having used
both hands, and rather
than face public scorn
sailed from Exmouth
one grey dawn
wrote up his log
tidily
then committed himself to the deep
suicidily.

Alf

Alf
on his day off from Billy Smart's,
tarts himself up. Puts on
his best monkey boots and braces
and races down to Clacton with his mates.
He hates so much it features
as a gruesome tattoo.
Pea-brained and circus-trained
a skinhead through and through.

Alf
is famous for his fighting skills
and rightly so.
He knocks out teeth with an entrechat
then pirouettes on his toe.
With a flick of the hip
and a backward flip
he blackens eyes. It's no surprise
he's the toast of the south coast

no butts about it.
He handstands on noses
then poses, so bold,
and his somersaults to the groin
are a joy to behold.

Alf
is an aggrobat.

Alfreda

His sister Alfreda
was somewhat gentler
(though some would argue
even mentler).

A juggler who would only juggle
with objects beginning with A
like acorns, armchairs and armadillos
alarm clocks and albatrosses
aspidistras, and one day
an alligator
which went straight for the juggler.

Cousin Fosbury

Cousin Fosbury
took his highjumping seriously.
To ensure a floppier flop
he consulted a contortionist
and had his vertebrae removed
by a backstreet vertebraeortionist.

Now he clears 8 foot with ease
and sleeps with his head
tucked under his knees.

Aunt Agatha

Aunt Agatha
blooded at five
loves to hunt foxes
and eat them alive.
No horsewoman,
she prefers to run
with the hounds.

On all fours
shod in running-
gloves and shoes,
no dog can match her
and once on the scent
nose smell-bent
no horse can catch her.

And she snaps
and she barks
and she urges the pack
onward on
to her bushy-tailed snack.

Tongue flapping
huntingpink suit
nostrils aflare
beware any hare
caught napping
en route.

And she snaps
and she barks
and she urges the pack
onward on
to her bushy-tailed snack.

D'ye ken Aunt Agatha
in her coat so gay
D'ye ken Aunt Agatha
at the close of day
houndsurrounded
tearing into foxflesh.

Old Mac

Old Mac, seventyodd
and eyes akimbo
was a prizefighter
in his youth.

Some nights in the bar
when he's had a few
he'll spar
with ghosts of pugilists
long since counted out.

Old Mac, still in training
for his final bout.

Eno

To be a sumo wrestler
　It pays to be fat.
'Nonsense,' said Eno,
　'I don't believe that.'

So he took his skinny
　little frame
to Tokyo
　in search of fame.

But even with God on
　his side
Eno got trod on
　and died.

Marvin

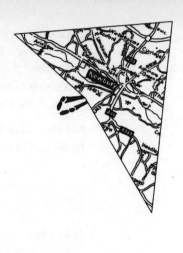

Never hangglide
with a hangover
as Marvin did
near Andover.

Dying for a whisky
to straighten his head
'Just one for the road'
is in fact what he said
Saw the pub on the left
turned right instead

Hit the M23 near the junction of the A303.

(Now, if he had turned left at the A34 he would have carried on to Newbury and swung a right at the A339 to Basingstoke. Alternatively, had he taken the A3057, he might have avoided the road works and then had the choice of reaching the M27 just south of Romsey, or coming off at the A30 and going straight through to Salisbury. Anyway, it's too late now, he's dead.)

Barry Bungee

Barry Bungee
who loved to dive
thrust himself upon fate
and didn't survive.

Life and death
it was just a game
To Bungee-jumping
gave his name.

The first and only
jump he made
was from City Hall
in Adelaide.

Securing the bungee
to the base
he scaled the building
at a leisurely pace.

And from the roof
hands on hips
surveyed a crowd
biting its lips

then jumped. The bungee
coiled like a garden hose.
Only the ground
kept its mouth closed.

Uncle Jason

Uncle Jason, an ace in the Royal Flying Corps
grew up and old into a terrible borps.
He'd take off from tables to play the Great Worps
stretch out his arms and crash to the florps.

His sister, an exSister (now rich) of the Porps,
would rorps forps morps: 'Encorps! Encorps!'

Cousin Christ

Cousin Christ (né Derek)
got out of bed at 8 to meditate.
Lacking a desert, he wandered
on Blackheath for 40 days
and 40 nights before being
arrested by two pharisees
in a panda car. 'Father,
forgive them,' he said.
And father, a door-to-door
used toupée salesman from Lewisham
did.

Cousin Fiona

Cousin Fiona
from near the top drawer
is a blueblood donor
and Kensington bore.

A moderate showjumper
plain and weakwilled
Cousin Fiona
is never fulfilled.

For what she wants
but will never admit
is a man to take her by the bit.

Someone to
jog with
snog with
look in her eyes
canter
banter
romanticize

Someone to
lead her
to pastures new
someone to
share her
pony-made-for-two.

UNDRESSAGE

And Fiona sleeps in a saddlesoaped room
and dreams of a pinstripe-jodhpured groom
and crop in hand, she gallops into moonlit gymkhanas
to ride gentleshod over her sinning nude
sinewed broncoing buck
giddyup giddyup giddy up up up.

And Fiona weeps after her lonely ride
always the bridle, never the bride.

Big Arth

Big Arth from Penarth
was a forward and a half.
Though built like a peninsula
with muscles like pink slagheaps
and a face like a cheese grater
he was as graceful and fast
as a greased cheetah.

A giraffe in the lineout
a rhino in the pack
he never passed forward
when he should've passed back
and once in possession
slaalomed his way
through the opposition.

And delicate?
Once for a lark
at Cardiff Arms Park
Big Arth
converted a softboiled egg
from the halfway line.

No doubt about it,
he was one of the best players in the second team.

Accrington Stan

A more talented footballer
    Never ran on a pitch
Than Accrington Stan
    Who might have been rich.

He could pass a ball
    He could score a goal
(But he couldn't pass a betting-shop
    So now he's on the dole).

The Hon. Nicholas Frayn

The Hon. Nicholas Frayn
who threw the javelin
would always travelin
a chauffeur-driven plane.
He somewhat lacked a chin
but always threw to win
and was notoriously vain.

He used only monogrammed javelins
sapphire-tipped and silver-plated
and was rated good enough to win his blue.
One day at a meeting in Crewe
he tripped and ran himself through
and though bleeding profusely
from a wound in his side
carried on gamely to finish next to last.
Then died.

Aunty Ann

Aunty Ann
an anti-angler
would dangle a
dead herring
on the end of a line.

A warning sign
to fishes
that man could be
vicious.

Not a popular figure
among the coarse
fishing crowd
she was found floating
one morning
in the river near Stroud.

At the memorial service
in an underwater church
the mourners were grayling
chub and perch,
salmon, pike and trout
who prayed, wet-eyed
then drifted out
to witness above
a heavenly banquet.

De profundis one by one
Temptation proved too great
Like angels falling into the sun
they rose, and took the bait.

Uncle Leo

Uncle Leo's sole ambition
was to be a liontamer
so he enrolled for classes at nightschool
and practised at home on his wife.

Aunt Elsa at first had reservations
but having once acquired
a taste for raw meat and the lash
she came on by leaps and bounds.

And after only 6 months
Uncle Leo announced with some pride
that his wife had opened her mouth
and he'd put his head inside.

One afternoon, however
while he was changing the sawdust
in the bathroom, Aunt Elsa escaped
mauled 2 boy scouts and a traffic warden
before being captured by the RSPCA.

Now a tamed Uncle Leo, give him his due
visits her daily at Regent's Park Zoo.

Uncle Len

Uncle Len
a redundant gamekeeper
strangled cuckoos.
He didn't give a f—whose

            c—oos

he strangled
as long as he silenced
as many as he could.

Last March in Bluebell Wood
while reaching for the season's
first feathered victim
he fell forty feet
broke his neck
and screaming,
unwittingly heralded spring.

Elmer Hoover

Elmer Hoover
on vac from
Vancouver
went fishing
off the Pier Head.

He caught 2 dead rats
dysentery
and a shoal of slimywhite balloonthings
which he brought home in a jamjar.
'Mersey cod,' we told him.

So he took the biggest
back to Canada.
Had it stuffed, mounted,
and displayed over the fireplace
in his trophy room.

'But you shudda seen
the one that got away,'
he would say.
Nonplussing his buddies.

Uncle Jed

Uncle Jed
Durham bred
raced pigeons
for money.

He died
a poor man
however

as the pigeons
were invariably
too quick for him.

Cousin Daisy

Cousin Daisy's
favourite sport
was standing
on streetcorners.

She contracted
with ease
a funny disease.
Notwithstanding.

Cousin Nell

Cousin Nell
married a frogman
in the hope
that one day
he would turn into
a handsome prince.

Instead he turned into
a sewage pipe
near Gravesend
and was never seen again.

Footy Poem

I'm an ordinary feller six days of the week
But Saturday turn into a football freak.
I'm a schizofanatic, sad but it's true
One half of me's red, and the other half's blue.

I can't make me mind up which team to support
Whether to lean to starboard or port
I'd be bisexual if I had time for sex
Cos it's Goodison one week and Anfield the next.

But the worst time of all is Derby day
One half of me's at home and the other's away
So I get down there early in me usual place
With me rainbow scarf and me two-tone face.

And I'm shouting for Liverpool, the Reds can't lose
'Come on de Everton' – 'Gerrin dere Blues'
'Use yer winger' – 'Worra puddin'
'King of der Kop' – All of a sudden – Wop!
'Goal!' – 'Offside!'

And after the match as I walk back alone
It's argue, argue all the way home
Some nights when I'm drunk I've even let fly
An given meself a poke in the eye.

But in front of the fire watchin' 'Match of the Day'
Tired but happy, I look at it this way:
Part of me's lost and part of me's won
I've had twice the heartaches – but I've had twice the fun.

Is My Team Playing

(after A. E. Housman)

Is my team playing
That I used to cheer
Each Saturday on the terrace
Before I transferred here?

Aye the lads still battle
They go from strength to strength
Won the FA Cup
Since you were laid at length.

Is factory still closed
With pickets at the gate?
Would I could lend a hand
Ere I felt the hand of Fate.

No things are back to normal
Thanks to the TUC
Our wages now are frozen
But not so much as thee.

And my lonely widow
Does she nightly grieve
For her dear departed
Gone early to the grave?

No she's right as rain
And not the one to weep
She is well looked after
Be still my lad, and sleep.

And what of you, dear friend
Are you still unwed
Or have you found a lady
To share your bachelor bed?

Well . . . er, I don't know how to say this
But after the funeral I got really plastered
I walked the widow back to yours, and

Oh, you lousy b*stard!

Poem for the opening of Christ the King Cathedral, Liverpool, 1967

O Lord on thy new Liverpool address
let no bombs fall
Gather not relics in the attic
nor dust in the hall
But daily may a thousand friends
who want to chat just call

Let it not be a showroom
for wouldbe good Catholics
or worse:
a museum
a shrine
a concrete hearse
But let it be a place
Where lovers meet after work
for kind words and kisses
Where dockers go of a Saturday night
to get away from the missus
Tramps let kip there through till morning
kids let rip there every evening

Let us pray there
heads held high
arms to the sky
not afraid and kneeling
let Koppites
teach us how to sing
God's 'Top of the Pops' with feeling

After visiting you
May trafficwardens let noisy parkers off
and policemen dance on the beat
Barrowomen knock a shilling off
exatheists sing in the street

And let the cathedral laugh
Even show its teeth
And if it must wear the cassock of dignity
Then let's glimpse the jeans beneath

O Lord on thy new Liverpool address
let no bombs fall
Keep always a light in the window
a welcome mat in the hall
That it may be a home sweet
home from home for all.

In Two Minds

What I love about night
              is the silver certainty of its stars
What I hate about stars
              is the overweening swank of their names
What I love about names
              is that every complete stranger has one
What I hate about one
              is the numerical power it wields over its followers
What I love about followers
              is the unseemly jostle to fill the footsteps
What I hate about footsteps
              is the way they gang up in the darkness
What I love about darkness
              is the soft sighing of its secrets
What I hate about secrets
              is the excitement they pack into their short lives
What I love about lives
              is the variety cut from the same pattern

What I hate about pattern
        is its dull insistence on conformity
What I love about conformity
        is the seed of rebelliousness within
What I hate about within
        is the absence of landscape, the feel of weather
What I love about weather
        is its refusal to stay in at night
What I hate about night
        is the silver certainty of its stars

crusader

in bed
like a dead
crusader

arms a
cross my chest
i lie

eyes closed
listening
to the body's glib mechanics

*   *   *

on the street
outside
men of violence

quarrel.
Their drunken voices
dark weals

on the
glistening
back of the night.

Catching up on Sleep

i go to bed early
to catch up on my sleep
            but my sleep
is a slippery customer
it bobs and weaves
            and leaves
me exhausted. It
side steps my clumsy tackles.
    with ease.   Bed
    raggled I drag
    myself to my knees.

The sheep are countless
I pretend to snore
yearn for chloroform
or a sock on the jaw
body sweats heart beats
there is Panic in the Sheets
until
as dawn slopes up the stairs
to set me free
unawares
sleep catches up on me

vampire

Blood is an acquired taste
'tis warm and sickly
and sticks to the teeth
a surfeit makes me puke.
I judge my victims as a connoisseur
a sip here, a mouthful there.
I never kill
and am careful to cause no pain
to those who sleeping nourish me
and calling once I never call again.

So if one morning you awake,
stretch, and remember
dark dreams of
                     falling
                     falling
if your neck is sore
a mark that wasn't there the night before
be not afeared 'tis but a sign
i give thee thanks
i have drunk thy wine.

warlock poems

(i)

when i fly
i keepclose
to chimneystacks and
gutted warehouses
hovering

just out of
reach of men's anger
i take off
from bombed-
sites and model
my tech-
nique on litter

caught

in

the

wind.
(During the day i camouflage myself
to blend against a thousand backgrounds
all grey)

my fear
is that one morn-
ing when i have landed
to re-
fuel with sadness
They
will capture me
tie my wings
behind my back
and drive a stake through my | fuselage

(ii)

on a clear night
some
stoned home re-
turner hearing a
cry, might gaze
upwards and see
me silhouett-
ed against the sky
trying vain
ly to get out
through the circular silver escape hatch

(iii)

i saw
            the hearse
                        coming towards me
            it was
                        too late
                                    to turn   back
                        when it
                                    drew level
                                                the coffin
shuddered
            and the bearers
                        had greatest
            difficulty   in keeping
                                    it under control
                        the crowd
                                    turned
                                                and saw me hiding
they pointed
            and shouted
                        and screamed
            everything
                        was black
                                    and purple
                        except
                                    the white faces
                                                advancing

i took to the air

Nocturne

Unable to sleep.
Every sound an enemy,
each stirring an intruder.

Even my own breathing
is frisked
before being allowed out.

I suffer during darkness
a thousand bludgeonings,
see blood everywhere.

How my poor heart
dreads the night
shift. I wear

a smear of sweat
like a moist plastercast.
Adrift in a monstered sea.

Those actors who scare so well
in your nightmares
have all practised first on me.

exsomnia

in bed
counting sheep
my attention
distracted by
a passing nude
when suddenly
a hoof
caught me
on the head
with a soft moan I collapsed

now i lie
by the bed
side more dead
than alive
waiting for the
somnambulance
to arrive

ofa sunday

ofa sunday
the only thing
i burn
at both ends
is my bacon.
Like the tele
.phone i am
off the hook

i watch the
newspapers for
hours & browse
through T.V.
miss mass
and wonder
if mass
misses me

italic

ONCE I LIVED IN CAPITALS
MY LIFE INTENSELY PHALLIC

but now i'm sadly lowercase
with the occasional *italic*

Scintillate

I have outlived
my youthfulness
So a quiet life for me.

Where once
I used to
scintillate

now I sin
till ten
past three.

Unlikely

It seems unlikely now
that I shall ever nod in
the winning goal for Everton
and run around Wembley with the cup.

Unlikely too
that I shall rout
the Aussies at Lords
with my deadly inswingers

that I shall play
the romantic lead in a Hollywood film
based on the Broadway musical
in which I starred

that I shall be a missionary
spreading wisdom
and the Word of God
amongst our pagan bretheren

it all seems unlikely now
and so I seek dreams more mundane
ambitions more easily attained

> a day at the seaside
> a poem started
> a change of beard
> an unruly orgasm
> a new tracksuit

and at the end of each day
I count my successes
(adding 10 if I go to bed sober)
by thus keeping one pace ahead of myself
I need never catch up with the truth

It seems unlikely now
that you will enter this room
close the curtains
and turn back the clock.

Waving at Trains

Do people who wave at trains
Wave at the driver, or at the train itself?
Or, do people who wave at trains
Wave at the passengers? Those hurtling strangers,
The unidentifiable flying faces?

They must think we like being waved at.
Children do perhaps, and alone
In a compartment, the occasional passenger
Who is himself a secret waver at trains.
But most of us are unimpressed.

Some even think they're daft.
Stuck out there in a field, grinning.
But our ignoring them, our blank faces,
Even our pulled tongues and up you signs
Come three miles further down the line.

Out of harm's way by then
They continue their walk.
Refreshed and made pure, by the mistaken belief
That their love has been returned,
Because they have not seen it rejected.

It's like God in a way. Another day
Another universe. Always off somewhere.
And left behind, the faithful few,
Stuck out there. Not a care in the world.
All innocence. Arms in the air. Waving.

Flying

from the ground
one sees only the arse end of clouds
those bits of the blanket
tucked under

Flying
one sees across the counterpane
rumpled, morning white,
as if the earth had spent
another restless night

Newsflash

In a dawn raid
early this morning
Gendarmes arrested
a family of four
found bathing
on a secluded beach
outside Swansea

Later in the day
tracker dogs
led German police officers
to the scene of a picnic
near Brighton.
Salmonpaste sandwiches
and a thermos of tea
were discovered.
The picnickers however
escaped.

Postcard

iceflow sighted
off Newquay
and they're surfing
in the High Street.
It's women and children first
in the T.V. lounge
and at lunchtime
there was an oilslick
in my soup
'Having a wonderful time
Wish you were her'

dawnmare on 24th St

talking
like we'd known eachother for years.
One hand on your heart
the other on my guitar
you pledge your troth.
A prostitute
takes a swing at someguy
with a ketchup bottle.
No one takes much notice
least of all the guy.

4 a.m. already.
Known eachother less than an hour
when I stumbled into the last ounce
of Paul Colby's party
(one of those Village Frontier scenes,
bagels, bangles and beans).
Someenchantedevening
acrossacrowdedroom etc.
I can't believe my luck.

Then you tell me you need heroin
and could I let you have seven dollars.
Together we go to the counter
and I pay 50 cents for the coffee.
As we leave, the prostitute screams
and reaches for the ketchup.
It's getting light.
I give you four dollars, all I have.
You kiss goodbye, no reason now to stay
i walk to my hotel, a poem's throw away.

Incident at a Presidential Garden Party

Taking tea in front of the White House.
Uninvited, a forty-ton diesel truck
Bursts through the railings
and skids across the lawn.

Tables are turned. Salads tossed
to the grass, canapés to the wind.
Colonels and creamcakes
squelch in the mad career.

Senators scream, tyres squeal,
underlings crunched underwheel.
Out of control, the juggernaut
surges towards the President.

No one moves. Slow motion now,
as in a dream. Half-smiling
he turns to face it. Smash.
Smithereens.   Then silence.

The Great Man dusts his suit
ensures his tie is straight.
The truck is given the kiss of life.
But too late.

There's Something Sad

There's something sad
about the glass
with lipstick on its mouth
that's pointed at and given back
to the waitress in disgust

Like the girl with the hair-lip
  whom
      no one
        wants
          to
            kiss.

What the Littlegirl Did

The littlegirl
  pulled up her bellyskin
      like a vest
        and examined her chest
          spleen, kidneys and the rest
            as a measled child a rash.

Sugar and spice
  and everything nice
      that's what littlegirls are made of

So she put in a hand
  and pulled out a gland
      and said: 'What a strange girl am I'

The horse's mouth

They bought the horse
in Portobello
brought it home
could hardly wait
installed it in the living room
next to knitted dinner plate

Next to ashtray
(formerly bedpan)
euphonium
no one can play
camel-saddle dollypeg
wooden gollywog with tray

Near a neo
deco lampshade
(a snip at
thirty-seven quid)
castanets and hula-hoop
trunk with psychedelic lid

Under front end
of a caribou
next to foam-
filled rollerskate
(made by a girl in Camden Lock
– she of knitted dinner plate)

Uprooted from
its carousel
the painted horse
now laid to waste
amidst expensive bric-à-brac
and sterile secondhand bad taste

*   *   *

And each night as Mr and Ms Trend
in brassbed they lie dreaming
the horse in downstairs darkness
mouths a silent screaming.

Poor Old Dead Horses

Don't give your rocking-horse
To the old rag and bony

He'll go straight to the knacker
And haggle for money

The stirrups are torn off
The bridle and harness

Chopped up for firewood
It is thrown on the furnace

And the water that boils
Is chucked down the sluices

To wash away what remains
Of poor old dead horses.

My Busconductor

My busconductor tells me
he only has one kidney
and that may soon go on strike
through overwork.
Each busticket
takes on now a different shape
and texture.
He holds a ninepenny single
as if it were a rose
and puts the shilling in his bag
as a child into a gasmeter.
His thin lips
have no quips
for fat factorygirls
and he ignores
the drunk who snores

and the oldman who talks to himself
and gets off at the wrong stop.
He goes gently to the bedroom
of the bus
to collect
and watch familiar shops and pubs passby
(perhaps for the last time?)
The sameold streets look different now
more distinct
as through new glasses.
And the sky
was it ever so blue?

And all the time
deepdown in the deserted busshelter of his mind
he thinks about his journey nearly done.
One day he'll clock on and never clock off
or clock off and never clock on.

My Busseductress

She is as beautiful as bustickets
and smells of old cash
drinks Guinness off duty
eats sausage and mash.
But like everyone else
she has her busdreams too
when the peakhour is over
and there's nothing to do.

A fourposter upstairs
a juke-box inside
there are more ways than one
of enjoying a ride.
Velvet curtains on the windows
thick carpets on the floor
roulette under the stairs
a bar by the door.

Three times a day
she'd perform a strip-tease
and during the applause
say nicely 'fares please'.
Upstairs she'd reserve
for men of her choice
invite them along
in her best clippie voice.

She knows it sounds silly
what would the police say
but thinks we'd be happier
if she had her way.
There are so many youngmen
she'd like to know better
give herself with the change
if only they'd let her.

She is as beautiful as bustickets
and smells of old cash
drinks Guinness off duty
eats sausage and mash.
But she has her busdreams
hot and nervous
my blueserged queen
of the transport service.

The Hippopotamusman

Into the world of the red glass bus
came a man with a face like a hippopotamus

Grotesqueeruptions made horrific
an otherwise normal ugly face
Wartsscrambled over his head
peeping between thin twigs of dry hair
like pink shiny sunsets
Hanging below the neckline
like grapes festering on a vine

And when he blinked
you could glimpse the drunken dance
in the whites of his eyes
like the flash of underpants
through unbuttoned trouserflies

Had the passengers been in groups
there might have been laughter
But they were all singles
and turning their faces to the windows
did not see the view
but behind the privacy of eyelids
had a mental spew

Limpinggropingly looking for a place
went the substandard man
with the hunchbacked face
and finding one sat
and beholding his mudstudded boots
the hippopotamusman
wondered whether it was wednesday.

The Icingbus

the littleman
with the hunchbackedback
creptto his feet
to offer his seat
to the blindlady

people gettingoff
steered carefully around
the black mound
of his back
as they would a pregnantbelly

the littleman
completely unaware
of the embarrassment behind
watched as the blindlady
fingered out her fare

* * *

muchlove later he suggested that instead
ofa wedding-cake they shouldhave a miniaturebus
made outof icing but she laughed
andsaid that buses werefor travelling in
and notfor eating and besides
you cant taste shapes.

Just another Autumn day

In Parliament, the Minister
for Mists and Mellow Fruitfulness
announces, that owing to
inflation and rising costs
there will be no Autumn
next year. September, October
and November are to be
cancelled, and the Government
to bring in the nine-month year instead.
Thus will we all live longer.

Emergency measures are to be
introduced to combat outbreaks
of well-being, and feelings
of elation inspired by the season.
Breathtaking sunsets will be
restricted to alternate Fridays
and gentle dusks prohibited.
Fallen leaves will be outlawed
and persons found in possession
of conkers, imprisoned without trial.
Thus will we all work harder.

The announcement caused little reaction.
People either way don't really care
No time have they to stand and stare
Looking for work or slaving away
Just another Autumn day.

The Last Strike

On Monday next
Undertakers are going on strike
Crematorium workers and gravediggers
Will be coming out in deepest sympathy

A state of emergency is to be declared
Soldiers who can be spared
From driving fire-engines, trains and bread vans
Will be called in to bury the dead

Throughout the country
There have been reports of widespread
Panic-dying

Conservative Government Unemployment Figures

Conservative Government.
Unemployment?
Figures.

Work-to-rule

Owing to an increase
in the cost of printing
this poem will be less
than the normal length.

In the face of continued
economic crises, strikes,
unemployment and V.A.T.
it offers no solutions.

Moreover, because of
a recent work-to-rule
imposed by the poet
it doesn't even rhyme.

The Leader

I wanna be the leader
I wanna be the leader
Can I be the leader?
Can I? I can?
Promise? Promise?
Yippee, I'm the leader
I'm the leader

OK what shall we do?

A Fair Day's Fiddle

Why can't the poor have the decency
to go around in bare feet?
Where's the pride that allows them
to fall behind on video recorders?

Such ostentation's indiscreet
when we can hardly afford as
much. They all smoke, of course,
and fiddle while the nation burns.

(Electric meters usually, and gas.)
And note, most have central heating.
Moonlighting's too romantic a word
for what's tantamount to cheating.

It's a question of priorities, I suppose,
give them money and it goes on booze.
Why can't the poor be seen to be poor?
Then we could praise the Lord, and give them shoes.

out of sequence

A task completed everyday
keeps sin and boredom both at bay
is what his mother used to say.

In a shop doorway
at the back of Skelhorne Street
a man in his early forties
grinning and muttering
is buttering a piece of bacon
with a pair of rusty scissors.
They are only nail scissors
and he has difficulty holding them
in his clumsy, larded hands.

The next day will be spent
untying the little knots.

In Renshaw Street
a man with blue eyes
and skin the colour of worn pavements
burrows into the busstop litterbin.
The sherrybottle is empty
but there is a bacon rasher
and a screwdup foil of Lurpak
as well as a deflated ball of string

String is great.
It ties up pillowends
and keeps the wind
out of your trouserlegs.

Things dont get lost
when there's string about.
Good to play with in bed.
Always keep some handy.

Near Windsor Street
where they are pulling down houses
there is much that rusts and glistens.
A pair of nail scissors
halfhidden by tin cans, stands,
one foot in the grave.
Approaching is a man
tying a rosary of knots into a length of dirty string.

His life, like this poem,
out of sequence,
a series of impressions,
unfinished, imperfect.

Unlucky for Some
13 voices from a woman's hostel in Soho, 1979

1

What do I do for a living? Survive.
Simple as that. 'God helps those
who help themselves.' That's what the
vicar told me. So I went into
the supermarket and helped myself.
Got six months. God help those
who help themselves. Nowadays
I'm a traveller. South-west mainly
then back here for the winter.
I like the open air. Plenty of it
and it's free. Everything else I beg
borrow or steal. Keep just about alive.
What do I do for a living? Survive.

2

It runs like duck's water off me back.
What people say. How do they know?
They seem to think I enjoy
looking shabby. Having no money.
Being moved on from cafés,
from warm places. How would
they like it? They'd soon sneer
on the other side of their faces
if they ended up down and out.
Up down and out. Up and down.
Out of luck. That's all you have to be.
Half of them calling the kettle black.
It runs like duck's water off me back.

3

It's the addicts I can't stand.
Getting drunk on pills. Stoned
they call it. Make me sick.
Sticking needles into themselves
in dirty lavatories. Got no shame.
And they get prescriptions. Wish
my doctor would give me one
everytime I felt like a drink.
I could take it along to the
allnight off-licence in Piccadilly
come back here and get drunk
for a week. Get high. Stoned.
It's the addicts I can't stand.

4

I'm no good, that's what I've been told
ever since I can remember. So
I try to live up to my reputation.
Or down to it. Thievin' mainly.
And drugs. You get used to prison.
Don't like it though, being cooped up.
That's why I couldn't work in a shop
or a factory. Drive me crazy.
Can't settle down. 21 years old
and I look 40. It's the drugs.
I'll O.D. probably. Couldn't care less.
Rather die young than grow old.
I'm no good, that's what I've been told.

5

Now I'm one of the idle poor.
A rose in a garden of weeds.
Slightly shrivelled of course, but nevertheless
an interesting species: '*Retrobata Inebriata*'.
I was born into the leisured classes.
No doubt you can tell. Born rich
and married rich as well. Too much
leisure that was the trouble. And drink.
Cost me a husband, home, family.
Now I've only a bed, a roof over my head.
Perhaps I don't deserve more.
I used to be one of the idle rich.
Now I'm one of the idle poor.

6

I get frightened you see. Easily scared.
Trouble is, I know what's goin' on.
The things they've got planned.
The others don't understand, you see.
They say: 'What are you scared of?
There's no need to be frightened.'
I huddle myself up against
the window sometimes. Like a curtain.
Listening to what's goin' on outside.
I've got X-ray hearin', you see.
It stretches for miles. When people
talk about me, I can hear every word.
I get frightened you see. Easily scared.

7

First and foremost I need a coat.
The one I'm wearing's got patches
on the patches. I can't go
for interviews dressed like this.
What sort of a job do you think
I'd get? A job as a tramp?
No thank you. And while I'm here
I need some vests and knickers.
None of them fancy ones either.
And shoes. Two pair. Leather.
Don't argue, I know my rights.
Refuse and I'll take you to court.
First and foremost I need a coat.

8

I try to take up little space.
Keep myself to myself. I find
the best way to get by is to say
nothing. Don't argue, don't interfere.
When there's trouble lie low.
That's why I wear a lot of grey.
Helps me hide away. Blend in
against the background. I eat
very little. Don't smoke or drink.
Get through the day unnoticed
that's the trick. The way to heaven.
Say me prayers each night just in case.
I try to take up little space.

9

It may sound silly but it's true.
I drink like there was no tomorrow
and I can't stand the taste of the stuff.
Never have. My mother was a drunk
and the smell of her was enough.
I drink to forget. I know it's a cliché
but it's true. I drink to forget
and I do. Occasionally I remember
what I was trying not to remember
but by then I've remembered
to drink, in order to make
myself forget. And I do.
It may sound silly but it's true.

10

I would have liked children I suppose.
A family and that. It's natural.
But it's too late now. Too old.
And trouble is I never liked men.
If I'd been born pretty
or with a nice figure, I might
have liked them then. Men,
and sex and that. But I'm
no oil painting. Had to face
that fact right from the start.
And you see, if you're born ugly
well that's the way life goes. But
I would have liked children I suppose.

11

Oh no, I don't have to be here.
I'm not a cast-off like the rest.
I'm one of the lucky ones. I've got
children. Both grown up. A son
and daughter who'd be only too pleased
to have me living with them.
But I prefer my independence.
Besides, they've got their own lives.
I'd only have to pick up the phone
and they'd be over. Or send money.
I mean, I could afford a room
in a nice clean hotel somewhere.
Oh no, I don't have to be here.

12

Things are better now with me new glasses.
I got the last pair just after the war
and I think they'd lost their power.
If I could read I'd be able
to read even better now. Everything's
so much clearer. Faces and places.
Television's improved too. Not
that I'm one for stayin' in.
I prefer to be out and about.
Sightseein' and windowshoppin'.
In and out of the traffic.
If you keep on the move, time soon passes.
Things are better now, with me new glasses.

13

I always wanted to go on the stage.
Dancer mainly, though I had a lovely voice.
Ran away to the bright lights of London
to be a star. Nothing came of it though,
so I went on the game. An actress
of sorts you might say. I'm the oldest
professional in the oldest profession.
Would you like to see me dance?
I'll dance for you. I dance in here
all the time. The girls love it.
Do you like my dancing? Round
and round. Not bad eh? For my age.
I always wanted to go on the stage.

The Lesson
A poem that raises the question:
Should there be capital punishment in schools?

Chaos ruled OK in the classroom
as bravely the teacher walked in
the havocwreakers ignored him
his voice was lost in the din

'The theme for today is violence
and homework will be set
I'm going to teach you a lesson
one that you'll never forget'

He picked on a boy who was shouting
and throttled him then and there
then garrotted the girl behind him
(the one with grotty hair)

Then sword in hand he hacked his way
between the chattering rows
'First come, first severed' he declared
'fingers, feet, or toes'

He threw the sword at a latecomer
it struck with deadly aim
then pulling out a shotgun
he continued with his game

The first blast cleared the backrow
(where those who skive hang out)
they collapsed like rubber dinghies
when the plugs pulled out

'Please may I leave the room sir?'
a trembling vandal enquired
'Of course you may' said teacher
put the gun to his temple and fired

The Head popped a head round the doorway
to see why a din was being made
nodded understandingly
then tossed in a grenade

And when the ammo was well spent
with blood on every chair
Silence shuffled forward
with its hands up in the air

The teacher surveyed the carnage
the dying and the dead
He waggled a finger severely
'Now let that be a lesson' he said

Water, Tree, Cave, Mother

This is the water
cold and black
that drowned the child
that climbed on its back

This is the tree
badtempered and tall
that tripped the child
and made it fall

This is the cave
with rotting breath
that hid the child
and starved it to death

This is the mother
who one day chose
to smother the child
with kisses, and blows and blows and blows.

Pantomime poem

'HE'S BEHIND YER!'
chorused the children
but the warning came too late.

The monster leaped forward
and fastening its teeth into his neck,
tore off the head.

The body fell to the floor
'MORE' cried the children
'MORE, MORE, MORE

MORE

Sleep Over

No, I'd rather stand, thank you. Sorry it's so late
but I wanted to get the girls settled down for the night.
Yes, they're sharing Emma's bedroom. Still awake, of course,
I could hear them chattering away as I slipped out.

Yes, I know they shouldn't be left alone in the house
that's why I want to get this business settled quickly.
I've brought over the film script you unwisely rejected.
The one about the producer whose daughter is kidnapped

by a psychopathic screenwriter. All you do is get it made.
You own the company, you're head of production.
Just do it. Naomi is a lovely kid. Hear what I'm sayin'?
Don't worry, I'll see myself out. Goodnight.

Persimmons

Watching the video last night was good.
The four of us stretched out on two sofas
after fish and chips. Lights dimmed.

Soon the heroine, a distracted single mum
with three kids in the red-neck South,
is in deep, deep trouble. Satanism.

Haddock, mushy peas and a large Sprite.
In her nightmare, someone is on the bed
trying to strangle her. She wakes in a sweat.

'*Pause*' to put the kettle on. The youngest
is happy to be put to bed. A story,
but only short because it is Saturday.

'*Play*.' As she hangs out the washing on the line,
her dead mother approaches with a basket of persimmons.
All the scarier for not being a nightmare.

My son is puzzled by the plum-like orange fruit,
and while discussing its taste and origins
we miss the psycho with the baseball bat.

'*Stop.*' '*Rewind?*' No, let her stay for ever
in the deep deep South. Eating forbidden fruit.
Hanging out the nightmares with her dead mother.

The Stranger

'Look quickly!' said the stranger
I turned around in time to see
a wall fall onto the child
playing beside a derelict house
In the silence of the rising dust
I saw the child's arm thrust
out stiff between the bricks
like a tulip

                    a white tulip

                              a clenched tulip

I turned angrily to the stranger
'Why did you have to tell me?'
'Well I thought you'd want to see' he said
the tulip screamed

                now limp

                            now red

snowscene

snow crackles underfoot
like powdered bones
trees have dandruff
in their hair
and the wind moans
    the wind moans

ponds are wearing glasses
with lenses three feet deep
birds are silent in the air
as stones
and the wind can't sleep
    the wind can't sleep

i found an oldman by the road
who had not long been dead
i had not heard his lonely groans
nor seen him weep
only birds heard the last words he said
before the wind pulled a sheet o'er his head
    the wind pulled a sheet o'er his head

The Wreck of the Hesperus

'You look like the wreck of the *Hesperus*
How long is it since you slept?'
As through the whistling sleet and snow
Like a sheeted ghost she swept.

'Where have you been until this hour
In roughest gale and stinging blast?'
Then wrapping her warm in his seaman's coat
He lay her down to rest.

'The least you could have done was ring
you knew I'd be worried sick.'
With rattling shrouds all sheathed in ice
She drifted, a dreary wreck.

'You promised on your mother's grave.
Why, oh why?' he cried.
But like the horns of an angry bull
The cruel rocks gored her side.

'Let me comb the seaweed from your hair
Come hither, daughter mine.'
But her brain was soft as carded wool
And her heart was caked with brine.

'Sleep tight,' said he. 'Sweet dreams,' said he,
'For soon the sun will rise.'
But the salt sea was frozen on her breast
The salt tears in her eyes.

Washed up was she, at break of day
(Christ save us all from a death like this)
On the bleak beach of the carpet lay
For she was the wreck of the *Hesperus*.
For she was the wreck of the *Hesperus*.

Closet fascist

in the staffroom
or over drinks
he says the things
with which he thinks
his colleagues will concur:
anti-Powell, anti-Front
liberalminded, fair.

But enthroned alone
in his W.C.
on toilet paper
signs a decree
deporting immigrants en masse.
Salutes the mob
then wipes his ass.

There are fascists

there are
fascists
pretending
to be
humanitarians

like
cannibals
on a health kick
eating only
vegetarians

Vegetarians

Vegetarians are cruel, unthinking people.
Everybody knows that a carrot screams when grated.
That a peach bleeds when torn apart.
Do you believe an orange insensitive
to thumbs gouging out its flesh?
That tomatoes spill their brains painlessly?
Potatoes, skinned alive and boiled,
the soil's little lobsters.
Don't tell me it doesn't hurt
when peas are ripped from the scrotum,
the hide flayed off sprouts,
cabbage shredded, onions beheaded.

Throw in the trowel
and lay down the hoe.
Mow no more
Let my people go!

There Was a Knock on the Door.
It Was the Meat.

There was a knock on the door.
It was the meat. I let it in.
Something freshly slaughtered
Dragged itself into the hall.

Into the living-room it crawled.
I followed. Though headless,
It headed for the kitchen
As if following a scent.

Straight to the oven it went
And lay there. Oozing softly to itself.
Though moved, I moved inside
And opened wide the door.

I switched to Gas Mark Four.
Set the timer. And grasping
The visitor by a stump
Humped it home and dry.

Did I detect a gentle sigh?
A thank you? The thought that I
Had helped a thing in need
Cheered me as I turned up the heat.

Two hours later the bell rang.
It was the meat.

Cabbage
(after 'I like that stuff' by Adrian Mitchell)

Humphrey Bogart died of it
People are terrified of it
                    cancer
                    I hate that stuff

Peter Sellers was laid low with it
one in five of us will go with it
                    heart attack
                    I hate that stuff

Monroe's life turned sour on it
Hancock spent his last half hour on it
                    sleeping pills
                    I hate that stuff

Jimi Hendrix couldn't wait for it
Chemistshops stay open late for it
                    heroin
                    I hate that stuff

Mama Cass choked on it
Blankets get soaked in it
                    vomit
                    I hate that stuff

Women learn to live with it
No one can live without it
                    blood
                    I hate that stuff

Hospitals are packed with it
Saw my mother racked with it
                    pain
                    I hate that stuff

Few like to face the truth of it
We're all living proof of it
                    death
                I hate that stuff

Schoolkids are forcefed with it
Cattle are served dead with it
                    cabbage
                I hate that stuff

Soil

we've ignored eachother for a long time
and I'm strictly an indoor man
anytime to call would be the wrong time
I'll avoid you as long as I can

When I was a boy we were good friends
I made pies out of you when you were wet
And in childhood's remembered summer weather
We roughandtumbled together
We were very close

just me and you and the sun
the world a place for having fun
always so much to be done

But gradually I grew away from you
Of course you were still there
During my earliest sexcapades
When I roughandfumbled
Not very well after bedtime
But suddenly it was winter
And you seemed so cold and dirty
That I stayed indoors and acquired
A taste for girls and clean clothes

we found less and less to say
you were jealous so one day
I simply upped and moved away

I still called to see you on occasions
But we had little now in common
And my visits grew less frequent
Until finally
One coldbright April morning
A handful of you drummed
On my father's waxworked coffin

at last it all made sense
there was no need for pretence
you said nothing in defence

And now recently
While travelling from town to town
Past where you live
I have become increasingly aware
Of you watching me out there.
Patient and unforgiving
Fidgeting with the trees.

we've avoided eachother for a long time
and I'm strictly a city man
anytime to call would be the wrong time
I'll avoid you as long as I can.

and the field screamed 'TRACTOR'

harvesttime
the sky
the inside of a giant balloon
sky blue
someone's yellow finger sticking through

late birds screech
wormless

waiting to be threshed
within an inch of its life
the field trembles

the pain
ohthepainoh
the pain

The Scarecrow

The scarecrow is a scarey crow
Who guards a private patch
Waiting for a trespassing
Little girl to snatch

Spitting soil into her mouth
His twiggy fingers scratch
Pulls her down on to the ground
As circling birdies watch

Drags her to his hidey-hole
And opens up the hatch
Throws her to the crawlies
Then double locks the latch

The scarecrow is a scarey crow
Always out to catch
Juicy bits of compost
To feed his cabbage patch

So don't go where the scarecrows are
Don't go there, Don't go there
Don't go where the scarecrows are
Don't go, Don't go . . .

Don't go where the scarecrows are
Don't go there, Don't go there
Don't go where the scarecrows are
Don't go . . .

The Birderman

Most weekends, starting in the spring
Until late summer, I spend angling.
Not for fish. I find that far too tame
But for birds, a much more interesting game.

A juicy worm I use as bait
Cast a line into the tree and wait.
Seldom for long (that's half the fun)
A commotion in the leaves, the job's half done.

Pull hard, jerk home the hook
Then reel him in. Let's have a look . . .
A tiny thing, a fledgling, young enough to spare.
I show mercy. Unhook, and toss it to the air.

It flies nestwards and disappears among the leaves
(What man roasts and braises, he too reprieves).
What next? A magpie. Note the splendid tail.
I wring its neck. Though stringy, it'll pass for quail.

Unlike water, the depths of trees are high
So, standing back, I cast into the sky.
And ledger there beyond the topmost bough,
Until threshing down, like a black cape, screams a crow!

Evil creature! A witch in feathered form.
I try to net the dark, encircling storm.
It caws for help. Its cronies gather round
They curse and swoop. I hold my ground.

An infernal mass, a black, horrific army
I'll not succumb to Satan's origami.
I reach into my coat, I've come prepared,
Bring out my pocket scarecrow – Watch out bird!

It's cross-shaped, the sign the godless fear
In a thunderflap of wings they disappear.
Except of course, that one, ungainly kite
Broken now, and quickly losing height.

I haul it in, and with a single blow
Dispatch it to that Aviary below.
The ebb and flow: magpie, thrush, nightingale and crow.
The wood darkens. Time to go.

I pack away the food I've caught
And thankful for a good day's sport
Amble home. The forest fisherman.
And I'll return as soon as I can

To bird. For I'm a birderer. The birderman.

The One About the Duck

This duck walked into a pub
and went straight up to the bar.
The barman made a joke about
not serving ducks under eighteen
and tried to shoo it out.

But the duck would not be shoon.
It waddled around to the back bar
quacking as it were last orders
to the few remaining customers
in the Sun Inn that afternoon.

So the barman fetched the barmaid
who tried to show the duck the door.
But the duck would not be shown.
So the barman fetched the manager,
but the three of them had no luck.

Seeking guidance from above, the manager
brought down the landlord and his wife,
and all five, armed with tea towels,
cornered the duck between the Ladies
and the fruit machine and overpowered it.

They were gentle, they were kind,
and their concern was for the welfare
of the web-footed intruder, the green-headed
alien away from his loved ones
and longing for home, Quack Quack.

So the landlord, followed by the landlady,
the manager, the barman and the barmaid
carried the duck, swaddled in tea towels,
across the High Street to the pond
that lies in the middle of the green.

'There you go, Donald, you naughty duck,'
said the landlord setting it free.
And his staff were pleased with their good deed,
and so, totally unprepared for the commotion
that followed. The sudden violence and murder.

Angels at four o'clock. While two fastened
on to its bill keeping it closed, the others
pecked and stabbed, turned it over
and dragged it under. Helpless, the rescuers
watched it drown in a bullseye of bubbles.

Stunned, they returned to the Sun
and tried to make sense of it all.
Synchronized drowning, bloodlust or justice?
Heads down, tails up, dabbling free.
Have you heard the one about the duck? No joke.

Honey and Lemon

Jogging around Barnes Common one April morning
when a rat crossed my path twenty metres ahead.
A fat, furry fist spelling danger from the tip
of its pointed nose to the end of its pointing tail.

Dogs daily, magpies frequently, rats? Never.
So, curious, I swerved left into the undergrowth
and took the overgrown path back to where
the beast (it had doubled in size) had scuttled.

Three strides along and there it was, barring
my way like a rival gang of football hooligans.
Red-eyed and snuffling, PLAGUE written all over it.
Motionless, I tried to stifle the fear rising within.

Having read in one of those survival handbooks
that rats love lemon, I spat the honey and lemon
pastille I was sucking straight into the bushes,
and sure enough, the brute dived in after it.

Unfortunately for the rat, a huge grizzly bear,
mad for honey, came crashing through the trees
and tore the creature to pieces with its iron claws.
By then, I was back on the road sprinting for home.

Five Ways to Help You Pass Safely through a Dark Wood Late at Night

1. Whistle a tune your father whistled
    when you were a child

2. Cross the first two fingers
    of your left hand

3. If you lose sight of the moon
    hold it in the mind's eye

4. Imagine the colours that surround you
    waiting for the first kiss of morning

5. Keep a Kalashnikov in the glove
    compartment

a cat, a horse and the sun

a cat mistrusts the sun
keeps out of its way
only where sun and shadow meet
it moves

a horse loves the sun
it basks all day
snorts
and beats its hooves

the sun likes horses
but hates cats
that is why it makes hay
and heats tin roofs

Trees Cannot Name the Seasons

Trees cannot name the seasons
Nor flowers tell the time.
But when the sun shines
And they are charged with light,
They take a day-long breath.
What we call 'night'
Is their soft exhalation.

And when joints creak yet again
And the dead skin of leaves falls,
Trees don't complain
Nor mourn the passing of hours.
What we call 'winter'
Is simply hibernation.

And as continuation
Comes to them as no surprise
They feel no need

To divide and itemize.
Nature has never needed reasons
For flowers to tell the time
Or trees put a name to seasons.

Sap

Spring again.
No denying the signs.
Rates bill. Crocuses on cue.
Daffodils rearing up
Like golden puff-adders.

Open to the neck, voices
Are louder. Unmuffled.
The lid lifted off the sky.
In the air, suddenly,
A feeling of '*je sais quoi*'.

I take the dog into the park.
Let myself off the lead.

Conservation Piece

The countryside must be preserved!
(Preferably miles away from me.)
Neat hectares of the stuff reserved
For those in need of flower or tree.

I'll make do with landscape painting
Film documentaries on TV.
And when I need to escape, panting,
Then open-mouthed I'll head for the sea.

Let others stroll and take their leisure,
In grasses wade up to their knees,
For I derive no earthly pleasure
From the green green rash that makes me sneeze.

Green Piece

Show me a salad
 and I'll show you a sneeze
Anything green
 makes me weak at the knees
On St Patrick's day
 I stay home and wheeze
I have hay fever all the year round.

Broken-down lawnmowers
 Bring me out in a sweat
A still-life of flowers,
 in oils, and I get
All the sodden signs
 of a sinus upset
I have hay fever all the year round.

A chorus of birdsong
 makes my flesh creep
I dream of a picnic
 and scratch in my sleep
Counting pollen
 instead of sheep
I have hay fever all the year round.

Summertime's great
 (except for the sun)
Holly and mistletoe
 make my nose run
Autumn leaves and I swoon
 it's no fun
Having hay fever all the year round.

Behemoth

Be he moth
or be he not
He be noth
ing when I swat

The Fly

I'm sorry, God, I cannot love
The fly
No matter how I try.

Floaters, bloated on dead flesh
And faeces
Lovers of the stale and the excreted
A species
I wish could be deleted.

I'm sorry, God, but why oh why
Did you create
The common fly?

Spiders I can abide when they approach
At a push, not crush a scuttling roach
But the fly I hate to bits.
Brings out in me a deathwish.
Its.

I'm sorry, God, I cannot lie
This morning I ✱ a fly.
And it felt good.

Crocodile in the City

The crocodile said to the cockatoo:
Cockatoo,
A croc's gotta do
What he's gotta do

The crocodile said to the chimpanzee:
Chimpanzee,
I want to be free
The jungle jangles not for me

The crocodile said to the mosquito:
Mosquito,
I must quit, oh,
I must admit, I just must go

The crocodile said to the koala bear:
Koala bear,
What are you doing up there?
ɐᴉlɐɹʇsn∀ uᴉ ǝq plnoɥs no⅄

The crocodile said to the parakeet:
Parakeet,
I'm stifled by this steamy heat
How I long to loll on a stone-cold street

The crocodile said to the alligator:
Alligator,
À *l'heure*, alligator, mate,
See you at a later date

The crocodile said to the piranha:
Piranha,
I leave for London *mañana*
Disguised as a giant banana

The crocodile said to the hippopotamus:
Sharon,
Give my love to Karen,
Gary, Wayne and Darren

Dear Mother

London cold Earth hard
Buildings giant into sky

To and fro menwo scarry
as if time on fire

At great noise cars speed
trailing bad breath

Crocodile keep to gutter
where slidder undisturbed

Dear Mother

Prisons underground
for rats are many found

Cats and dogs cowed
kowtow to menwo

Birds are not radiant
nor celebrate lives in song

Are pavement-coloured
and scream

Dear Mother

During daylight sightsee See
sights for sore eyes

See eyesores soar
So far have sightseen

Buckingham Palace Tower
Bridge Houses of Parliament

Yesterday went to Madame Tussaud's
and ate lots of famous people

Dear Mother

Night is best Moonlight
become crocodile

Stars dance in scales
asa hunting go

Late home-returner
beware puddle that move

Beware reflection that salivate
Moonlight that become crocodile

Dear Mother

Arched in pain
on pavement

Throat dry
as parchment

Parched
thirst saharan

Water water
sting of carbreath

Dear Mother

London hard Earth cold
Too tired now to hunt meat

Eat Coke cans McDonald's cartons
Kentucky fried chicken boxes

Water is black Like swallowing
putrid snake Cannot see

Tongue is swollen Head is burning
Tomorrow crocodile return home

Kentucky fried snake

home is cold carton

chicken is swollen water

mother is putrid meat

earth is dear

coke is hard

McDonald's is tired now

head is black box

tongue is swallowing

London is burning

crocodile cannot see

tomorrow

The Lake

For years there have been no fish in the lake.
People hurrying through the park avoid it like the plague.
Birds steer clear and the sedge of course has withered.
Trees lean away from it, and at night it reflects,
not the moon, but the blackness of its own depths.
There are no fish in the lake. But there is life there.
There is life . . .

Underwater pigs glide between reefs of coral debris.
They love it here. They breed and multiply
in sties hollowed out of the mud
and lined with mattresses and bedsprings.
They live on dead fish and rotting things,
drowned pets, plastic and assorted excreta.
Rusty cans they like the best.
Holding them in webbed trotters
their teeth tear easily through the tin
and poking in a snout
they noisily suck out
the putrid matter within.

There are no fish in the lake. But there is life there.
There is life . . .

For on certain evenings after dark
shoals of pigs surface and look out
at those houses near the park.
Where, in bathrooms, children feed stale bread to plastic ducks
and in attics, toyyachts have long since runaground.
Where, in livingrooms, anglers dangle their lines
on patterned carpets, and bemoan the fate
of the ones that got away.

Down on the lake, piggy eyes glisten.
They have acquired a taste for flesh.
They are licking their lips. Listen . . .

Curse

Cyanide in the forest
Dead fish in the sea
A loaded gun
Where the sun should be

May those who sold us
Down the river
As polluted
As the lies they told

Find their banknotes
Carcinogenic
Nuclear active
Their gold.

Pure Jaguar
*Cut-up of a wildlife conservation leaflet and a sales brochure
for Jaguar Motors*

Dark clouds. The fresh smell of new rain. The soft hiss
of rubber on smooth, wet bitumen. A reflection in a window:
*a powerful, deep-chested, stocky cat with a large rounded
head and short sturdy limbs.* This is the most technically
well-endowed road-going jaguar yet.

*The fur varies from pale gold to a rich, rust red,
and is patterned with a series of dark rosettes
that enclose one or two smaller spots.* The body
isn't just stunningly handsome, it's also 30% stiffer
on twist than the previous class leader.

*Being good climbers, jaguars often rest in trees,
but are believed to hunt almost entirely on the ground.*
That makes it a superb platform from which to mount
an extraordinarily supple, yet at the same time,
tightly controlled suspension package.

Using urine, tree scratches and calls to mark their boundaries
jaguars are not, and never will be commonplace.
A jaguar is special and the X-type is more special still.
It will feed on almost anything including lizards, snakes,
turtles, front, side and curtain airbags.

The jaguar's powerful jaws, robust canine teeth,
and the cool integrity of sculptured steel, *enable it*
to kill livestock weighing 3 or 4 times its own weight,
often with a bite to the back of the skull. The ambience
that is, quite simply, pure jaguar.

Five-car Family

We're a five-car family
We got what it takes
Eight thousand cc
Three different makes

One each for the kids
I run two
One for the missus
When there's shopping to do

Cars are Japanese of course
Subaru and Mazda
And the Nissan that the missus takes
Nippin down to Asda

We're a load of noisy parkers
We never do it neat
Drive the neighbours crazy
When we take up half the street

Unleaded petrol?
That's gotta be a joke
Stepping on the gas we like
The smoke to make you choke

Carbon monoxide
Take a deep breath
Benzine dioxide
Automanic death

'Cos it's all about noise
And it's all about speed
And it's all about power
And it's all about greed

And it's all about fantasy
And it's all about dash
And it's all about machismo
And it's all about cash

And it's all about blood
And it's all about gore
And it's all about oil
And it's all about war

And it's all about money
And it's all about spend
And it's all about time
That it came to an end.

Stop All the Cars
(The Metro, 1980–1998, RIP)

Stop all the cars, cut off the ignition
Those who decide have made the decision
Muffle the exhaust, put flowers in the boot
Wear a black dress or a morning suit.

Let the traffic lights remain on red
Jam the horns out of respect for the dead
Sound the Last Post and summon the guard
For the Metro has gone to the knacker's yard.

She was my rustbucket, my tin lizzie
She kept my garage mechanic busy
A tarnished icon of the Thatcher years
She ground to a halt as I ground the gears.

Traffic wardens openly break down and weep
Sleeping policemen stir in their sleep
Car thieves consider an easier trade
Ram-raiders can't be bothered to raid.

Close the motorways with black-ribboned cones
Riddle the ashes and rattle the bones
Sound the Last Post and summon the guard
For the Metro has gone to the knacker's yard.

Stinging in the Rain

Stinging in the rain	I'm
Stinging in the rain	My
Skin is peeling	I'm
Stinging in the rain	I
Don't like feeling	I
Can't stand the pain	It's
Burning my flesh	And
Boiling my brain	The
Buildings are melting	I
Can't take the strain	There's
Blood on the sidewalk	I'm
Going insane	I'm
Crying and frying	And
Dying in vain	I'm
Stinging just stinging	
In the stinking acid	
(What a glorious feeling . . .	

The City of London Tour

'Along Leadladen Street
Into Snarl-up Close
Through Crosspatch
Into Coronary Circus

Past Foulmouth Gardens
Into Fetid Lane
Along Profligate
To the station at Charnel House

Up Dirtneedle Street
Into Destitute Square
Down Pacemaker Passage
(Nearly there)

A quick one in the "Half Lung"
(Leave your gasmask at the door)
Which concludes, ladies and gents,
The City of London Tour.'

Sheer

Cliff faces do not like the word 'sheer'
Especially those who are afraid of heights.
One day, you are a rising upland,
a grassy ridge overlooking vales and hills
that roll gently toward the distant sea

And the next, the distant sea has crept up
behind you. A crack, an ice-pick
into the skull of your nearest and dearest
and there you are, thrust to the fore,
up to your knees in stinging foam.

Don't look down. Keep your eyes fixed
on the horizon. Ignore the squealing,
dizzy flight of gulls. The squalls,
the gales that smack, the nails that scratch.
An era or two and you'll get used to it.

Even come to enjoy your position. Looked up to
and admired, surveyed and photographed.
Until, when you least expect it, the earth sighs,
a fractal blip, and you sheer away into the sea.
Today, a proud headland, tomorrow, oceanography.

On Dover Beach

For one magical moment you imagine
you are at the wheel of a moon-blanch'd
powerboat, speeding across a calm sea
towards the white cliffs of Dover.

But no, you are here on the darkling plain
powerless, as it comes roaring in.
You shout its name into the wind:
'Tsunami, Tsunami', over and over.

Global Warming

In the Antarctic, an ice-shelf
Twice the size of Norfolk
Has broken off, and is melting.

People the world over are concerned
Especially those in Suffolk
Who always get the thin end of the wedge.

Fatal Consequences

I don't believe that one about the butterfly –
The air displaced by the fluttering
of its wings in Brazil
causing a tidal wave in Bangladesh.

Mind you,
The day after I shook out
a tablecloth on the patio
there was an earthquake in Mexico.

(Or was it the other way round?)

Bad Day at the Ark

On the eleventh morning
Japheth burst into the cabin:
'Dreadful news, everybody, the tigers
have eaten the bambanolas!'

'Oh, not the bambanolas,' cried Mrs Noah.
'But they were my favourites,
all cuddly and furry,
and such beautiful brown eyes.'

Noah took her hand in his.
'Momma, not only were they cute
but they could sing and dance
and speak seven languages.'

'And when baked, their dung was delicious,'
added Shem wistfully.
Everybody agreed that the earth
would be a poorer place without the bambanolas.

Noah determined to look on the bright side.
'At least we still have the quinquasaurapods.'
'Oh, yes, the darling creatures,' said his wife.
'How would we manage without them?'

On deck, one quinquasaurapod was steering,
cooking, fishing, doing a crossword
and finding a cure for cancer.
The other was being stalked by a tiger.

Bad Day at the Ark (II)

One evening while the family were at vespers
From the deck came the sound of furtive whispers.

Impatiently, Ham waited for 'Amen'
Then crept up to investigate with Shem.

Like phantoms in the moonlight, glistening with slime
Two giant slugs were ranting, horns swaying in time:

Sluggy deluge sluggy dark, Sluggy voyage sluggy ark
Sluggy seasick sluggy sneeze, Sluggy splinters sluggy fleas
Sluggy Noah sluggy wife, Sluggy boring sluggy life

Each feculent slug was as huge as a rhino
And smelled of old corpses rolled up in lino.

Clammy, putrescent, oozing mucus and goo
The Creator's revenge locked one night in the loo.

Sluggy bellow sluggy bleat, Sluggy twitter sluggy tweet
Sluggy roar sluggy meow, Sluggy bow sluggy wow
Sluggy quack sluggy moo, Sluggy sink the sluggy crew

'Not only ugly, out of tune and glutinous
These beasts are revolting,' said Shem, 'and mutinous.

Let's do the deed and do it big time
You get the sea-salt, I'll get the quick-lime.'

Sluggy quick-lime, sluggy salt, Sluggy human's sluggy fault
Sluggy melting, sluggy pain, Endangered species down the drain
No one loves a sluggy slug, Gluggy gluggy glug glug glug

Noah, on hearing of the creatures' cruel demise,
Summoned his sons and frowning said, 'Now guys

Our job is to save life, so you're way off the mark
To make a floating abattoir out of an ark.

This cannot go unpunished, and so tonight,
No custard with your apple pie, all right?

Let that be a lesson,' adding with a smirk,
'Giant slugs? Good riddance. Now get back to work.'

Bad Day at the Ark (III)

'They've struck again,' said Mrs Noah, disconsolate.
'A Duck-billed Reindeer this time.
A doe. She had no chance, poor mite.
Sucked dry and covered in pollen,
she lay on deck like a squeezed shammy leather,
little Bambi, whimpering at her side.'

'Those Killer Butterflies will have to go,'
said Noah. 'With a wing-span of twelve metres
and heads the size of mammoths,
they are a liability to everyone on board.
Compared to these Cabbage White vampires
the Giant Bees were pussycats.'

'And functional,' pointed out his wife,
squeezing her toes into the luxurious pile
of the black and yellow striped carpet.
'Mind you, those diaphanous wings
would make a smashing pair of window-blinds
for the nursery. Shall I give the lads a call?'

She picked up the skull of a ring-tailed
maraca and shook it vigorously.
Ham, Shem and Japheth came running,
armed to the back teeth and clad
in the bright red armour of the recently boiled
(and now extinct) Giant Lobsters.

'Death to the blood-sucking lepidoptera,'
they cried (in Hebrew), and ran on deck.
But the beasts were nowhere to be seen.
Having mistaken the distant horizon
for a washing-line, they had fluttered off
to perch upon it and perished. (Honest.)

So Mrs Noah did not get the window-blinds
she had set her heart on for the nursery.
But, by way of compensation, her husband
made a fine set of rockers for the cot
using a pair of gleaming ivory tusks
taken from a Giant Sabre-toothed Hamster.

Bad Day at the Ark (IV)

It occurred first to the lemon-haired manatee
(sole survivor of a pair of poolside-dwelling bipeds)
as she and a male barefaced baboon
were in hiding from Shem, who, armed with a carving-knife
fashioned from the horn of a unicorn, was scouring the ship
in search of something tasty and intelligent for supper.

'If this voyage lasts much longer,' she whispered,
'there will be no animals left to do God's bidding
once the flood subsides.' The baboon nodded,
letting his hand fall on to the silken flesh of her thigh.
The manatee removed his hand gently but firmly.
'I think we should call a meeting, don't you?'

The survivors convened that same night in the empty
brontosaurus basket, and what a sorry sight they were:
Gone the fabulous gryphon, the wingèd giraffe.
Gone the prairie dolphin, the golden-voiced terrapin.
'I hate to say this,' confessed the manatee,
'but I really think that God messed up on this one.

To entrust the infamous Noahs with the task
of building an ark and leading us all to safety
was asking for trouble. I mean, just look at them:
purple-scaled, one-eyed, cloven-hoofed non-entities.
They can talk, yes, and they're house-trained
but in terms of evolution they're . . . they're . . .'

She looked to the barefaced baboon for inspiration.
He winked and wiggled his long tongue lasciviously
'. . . they're way down the line.' The animals yelped,
roared and belched in approval. 'We must jump ship
before reaching dry land, otherwise they'll carry on
where they left off, and consume us at the rate of knots.'

As if on cue, the wind dropped suddenly, and the rain
pitter-petered out. 'It has to be tonight,' she warned.
While the baboon and a few of his best primates
barricaded the Noahs into their sleeping-quarters,
the upturned shell of a blue turtle-whale was lowered
upon the now calm waters, boarded and sailed away.

The Ark and all therein perished, but the giant shell
was washed safely ashore, its precious cargo intact.
The animals gave thanks, and then wearily but joyfully
set off to the four corners of the earth to breed and multiply.
And last to leave were the new Adam and Eve –
The lemon-haired manatee and the barefaced baboon.

St Francis and the Lion

The man was sick. He had a history
of mental illness. What he was doing
let loose on the streets we'll never know.
Care in the community they call it.
Wild animals, of course, couldn't care less.

During the summer months the zoo closes
at 8 p.m. It is possible that he got in
after that by scaling the perimeter fence,
but more likely he was already inside,
hiding away, when the keepers locked up.

The lion compound is encircled by a low wall,
a ditch, and a fence seven metres high,
enough to deter even the most athletic
trespasser. The man, however, appears
to have had no trouble in scaling it.

Whether this was a dramatic suicide attempt
or whether he believed he had an empathy
with the beasts is anybody's guess.
Although conclusions may be drawn from the fact
that he was wearing sandals and carrying a Bible.

The victim, who was in his early twenties,
has yet to be identified. Cause of death
would appear to be a broken neck.
The injury consistent with receiving
a single blow from a fully grown male lion.

St Francis and the Lion (II)

We haven't spoken to him since that evening.
As far as we're concerned he's burned his boats.
At first he was all bravado
Trying to justify himself. But it didn't wash.

He knew right away that he'd let us down.
From now on he's on his own
and serves him right. Everybody is upset,
especially the young ones. Let him stew.

We knew that it was St Francis
as soon as he opened his mouth.
He spoke in our language, and beautifully.
Words that were music, that could dance.

But Mali was jealous right from the start.
Yawning, scratching and wandering off,
pretending not to listen. But he did.
You couldn't help but be impressed.

He talked about love and about God
and about how one day, all the fences
would come down and we'd be free
to run wild for ever and ever.

It was then that the devil got into him.
We don't know if it was fear or anger
but whatever it was, he suddenly
let out a roar and sprung upon the boy.

It was over before any of us could move.
No screams. No cries for help.
Motionless he lay. The sun loosening
its grip on the iron bars of the cage.

I suppose, in time, Mali will be forgiven
and he'll return to the pride when the memory
has faded. Already the cynics are whispering . . .
'Mass hysteria . . . Hallucination . . . Once upon a time . . .'

The Father, the Son

It is unusual to find me here, in town.
I never did like crowds. The smell,
The dust, the racket. I can do without it.
But it's a special occasion, and well,
I haven't seen him in a long, long time.

Followed his career with interest, mind.
Well, hardly career, but he's made his mark
They all have, and good on them I say.
The whole country needs shaking up
And they're the boys to do it.

Things are coming to a head now.
History in the making, you can sense it.
That's why I'm here. I may be old
But not too old to lend a hand
Lift a sword and strike a blow for freedom.

Question is, when push comes to shove
Will they stand and fight, or run for it?
They'll not fight alone, that's for sure.
The rank and file will rally round
Even though the odds are stacked against.

Too many leeches with too much to lose
The mobsters, the spies, the black marketeers.
Too many fingers in too many pies.
The backhanders, the sweeteners, the graft
The wheeler-dealers, the sultans of sleaze.

The ones who feed on the carrion of conflict
Who profit from the status quo
Who fuel the hatreds that keep
The tribes apart. Who know
That where there's fear, there's money.

Unless this Jesus can provide the glue
By all accounts he knows a thing or two.
Peace is what he preaches. A coded message
That's clear to understand: There'll be no peace
Until Rome has been driven from this land.

And my son knows that. That's why
He got involved. To fight for the cause.
A chip off the old block and no mistake.
But smarter. Not like his old man, hot-headed.
He likes to plan. Take stock. Cool in a crisis.

Ah, there's something happening now.
Can you hear the cheering? It must be them.
The crowd is ecstatic, and the soldiers,
Under orders, keeping out of the way.
Nervous too, a good sign that, I'd say.

But where's my lad? Ah, there he is
At the back, following at a slower pace.
Looks strangely downcast, I must confess.
But no doubt the sight of his old dad
Will bring a smile to his face . . .
'Judas! . . . Judas!'

Tsutsumu

Tsutsumu: The Japanese art of wrapping items in an attractive and appropriate way.

Dear Satoshi,
Thank you for the egg. Smashed in transit, I'm afraid.
The origami chicken that it came in, however,
although gooey was exquisite. How clever you are!

We hesitated for ages before gently dismantling
the Taj Mahal. Perhaps now we regret it.
My wife is over the moon with the curry powder.

It seemed a shame to unpick the delicate spinning-wheel.
Straight out of an enchanted castle, we thought!
The plastic thimble will surely come in handy.

The walnut tree was so lifelike
we considered replanting it in our little garden.
Thank you for the walnut.

And that salmon! The magic you weave with paper!
It seemed to shimmer with life and jump for joy.
Sadly the slice of sashumi was well past its sell-by.

When the life-size model of a Toyota Landcruiser
was delivered, we were as tickled as the postman!
Our thanks for the jasmine-scented car-freshener.

Finally, a note of apology.
It was only after we had broken the string,
torn off the paper, and smashed open the box,
that we realized we had destroyed your gift
of a beautiful box. Sorry.

Spoil-sports

There's always someone who spoils things, isn't there?
We are all enjoying the story
and someone has to shout out something silly.

We are all there in good time
and someone has to be late
spoiling it for everybody else.

There we are, all dressed up, gone to a lot of trouble
and someone had to show up
looking like I don't know what.

They do it on purpose, we know that.
Just to make themselves feel important.

When not destroying plant-life
they're using sawn-off shotguns.
Blowing up aeroplanes
Not paying their TV licences
Throwing my satchel into the canal
Reporting me to Mr Clark, and I hadn't done anything.

*   *   *

My wife and I run a little business.
Exotic plants. Carnivores mainly. Venus flytraps,
that sort of thing. The place is always full
and we take the time to explain how,
once trapped within the plant, the insects
are broken down by enzymes and the proteins
extracted, leaving only the decaying husks.
People find it fascinating, especially children.

But as soon as your back is turned
there is always someone who thinks it's funny
to introduce foreign bodies. Chewing-gum,
sweet-wrappers, lolly-ice sticks, pencils,
even a chicken tikka sandwich once.

They do it on purpose, we know that.
Just to be different, just to spoil it for everybody else.

Pen Pals

As you can imagine, a man in my position
Receives a lot of mail. My poor wife, on the other hand,
None at all. Until recently that is

When the postman dropped her a line.
His motives, I am sure, were altruistic,
And her reply, written that same morning,

Prompted by feelings of courtesy.
His letter by return, however, was ripped open
In a manner that could be regarded as unseemly.

And when my wife took breakfast
Locked in her room, composing a reply
I should have spotted the danger signals.

But, being absorbed in various projects, did not.
In fact, I delighted at seeing her fulfilled,
The loose ends of her days gummed down.

It was BURMA at the beginning of the third week
That set the alarm bells ringing. Although
Not widely travelled, I am a man of the world.

And the thought of My Angel, Being Undressed
And Ready for Postman Pat spurred me into action.
Our nearest pillar-box is at the end of the road

And that morning I crouched behind it, until,
Just before noon, she approached, the ink not yet dry.
And as she offered the profane wafer to its iron lips

I leaped out and snatched it from her grasp.
In the privacy of my rooms I tore open the letter
And confronted her with its contents.

'Pen pals,' she insisted. 'We are only pen pals.'
'Pen pals,' I pointed out, 'don't make plans
To cavort in the back of Delivery Vans.'

I insisted that the relationship be terminated
Immediately, and dictated the following:
'Dear Ken,' (for Ken it was)

'I wish to break off this ludicrous affair,
This adultery-by-proxy. I will have my revenge
You bastard. Yours, Audrey' (for Audrey it was)

'P.S. Another letter to follow.'
I made her post it that same afternoon
And next morning I posted the letterbomb.

The sorting office was out of action for several days
And my wife arrested the following Monday.
But now, thankfully, everything is back to normal.

Old-fashioned Values

I have old-fashioned values
Prefer things the way they used to be
When good manners were a premium
And there was a sense of community

Front doors could be left wide-open
And children play out in the street
Everyone on first-name terms
With the bobby on his beat

No beggars huddled in doorways
No muggers in the dark
No syringes in the stairwells
No rapists in the park

On a crowded bus a man would stand
To offer a lady his seat
Vegetables came fresh from the land
There was gravy and innocent meat

No holes in the ozone layer
No AIDS or BSE
No serial killers in Gloucester
No violence on TV

I have old-fashioned values
Prefer things the way they used to be
When the world wore a smile
And I was young, in nineteen eighty-three.

Light Sleeper

My wife is such a light sleeper
That when I come home late
After a night out with the boys
I always remove my shoes
And leave them at the bottom
Of the street.

Imagine my surprise, when
On retrieving them this morning
I discovered that they had been
Polished.

What a nice neighbourhood I live in.
What a great country this is.

Ex Patria

After supper, we move out on to the veranda.
Moths flit between lamps. We drink, think about sex
and consider how best to wreck each other's lives.

At the river's edge, the kitchen maids are washing up.
In the age-old tradition, they slap the plates
against the side of a rock, singing tonelessly.

Like tiny chauffeurs, the mosquitoes will soon arrive
and drive us home. O England, how I miss you.
Ascot, Henley, Wimbledon. It's the little things.

Posh

Where I live is posh
   Sundays the lawns are mown
My neighbours drink papaya squash

Sushi is a favourite nosh
   Each six-year-old has a mobile phone
Where I live is posh

In spring each garden is awash
   with wisteria, pink and fully blown
My neighbours drink papaya squash

Radicchio thrives beneath the cloche
   Cannabis is home grown
Where I live is posh

Appliances by Míele and Bosch
   Sugar-free jam on wholemeal scone
My neighbours drink papaya squash

Birds hum and bees drone
   The paedophile is left alone
My neighbours drink papaya squash
Where I live is posh.

Shite

Where I live is shite
   An inner-city high-rise shack
Social workers shoot on sight

The hospital's been set alight
   The fire brigade's under attack
Where I live is shite

Police hide under their beds at night
   Every road's a cul-de-sac
Social workers shoot on sight

Girls get pregnant just for spite
    My mate's a repo-maniac
Where I live is shite.

Newborn junkies scratch and bite
    Six-year-olds swap sweets for crack
Social workers shoot on sight

Tattooed upon my granny's back
    A fading wrinkled Union Jack
Social workers shoot on sight
Where I live is shite.

The Jogger's Song

After leaving the Harp nightclub in Deptford, a 35-year-old woman
was raped and assaulted by two men in Fordham Park. Left in a
shocked and dishevelled state she appealed for help to a man in a
light-coloured tracksuit who was out jogging. Instead of rescuing
her, he also raped her.

Standard, 27 January 1984

Well, she was asking for it.
Lying there, cryin out,
dying for it. Pissed of course.
Of course, nice girls don't.
Don't know who she was,
where from, didn't care.
Nor did she. Slut. Slut.

Now I look after myself. Fit.
Keep myself fit. Got
a good body. Good body. Slim.
Go to the gym. Keep in trim.
Girls like a man wiv a good body.
Strong arms, tight arse. Right
tart she was. Slut. Pissed.

Now I don't drink. No fear.
Like to keep a clear
head. Keep ahead. Like
I said, like to know what I'm doin
who I'm screwin (excuse language).
Not like her. Baggage. Half-
dressed, couldn't-care-less. Pissed.

Crawlin round beggin for it.
Lying there, dyin for it.
Cryin. Cryin. Nice girls don't.
Right one she was. A raver.
At night, after dark,
on her own, in the park?
Well, do me a favour.

And tell me this:
If she didn't enjoy it,
why didn't she scream?

Fart

He was lyin there, so I . . . er
Stabbed him. Just the once.
In the stomach. Crashed out
on the sofa he was. After the pub.

He wasn't asleep. Some nights
he'd pass out but most nights he'd pretend.
Lie there he would, eyes closed.
Burp. Fart, like I wasn't there.

Eggin me on to say somethin.
And if I did. If ever I did,
you know, say what I thought
He'd be up in a flash.

Because that's what he wanted
Me to say somethin. Lose my temper.
I'd goaded him, you see. Asked for it.
'You asked for it,' he'd say

Afterwards, in bed, me, sobbin.
A fresh bruise on an old swellin.
Not on the face. He never hit me
on the face. Too calculatin.

Always the body. Stomach, kidneys
He used to be one of you, see.
He knew where to hit.
Cold. Always, in control.

But tonight, I took control.
Picked up the breadknife.
He was gettin ready to let one go
I could see that.

The veins in his neck standin out
Throbbin. White against the purple.
Eyes behind closed lids, flickerin
Waitin to jump out on me.

So I . . . er stabbed him. Just the once.
He farted and screamed at the same time.
I know that sounds funny, but it wasn't
Not at the time. Not with the blood.

He rolled off of the sofa
Hunched on his knees, holdin the knife.
Not trying to pull it out
Just holdin it. Like keepin it in.

Then he keeled over and that was that.
I put my coat on and came down here
And what I want to know is . . .
What's goin to happen to the kids?

End of Story

Sometimes I wish I was back in Nicosia
smoking the wacky-backy with the lads
and watching Sandy getting tarted up.

Night on the town. Blood on the streets.
Razor-blades stitched into the lapels
of his crushed-velvet tartan jacket.

Headcase but funny with it. Not like Fitzy.
Now we're talking nasty bastards.
Four brothers and half a brain between them.

He only knew three questions:
Who are you lookin at? What did you say?
Are you takin the piss?

Simple questions that no one ever got right
because only Fitzy knew the answers:
(a) Beerglass (b) Boot (c) Head-butt.

Put on more charges than the Light Brigade.
Next thing, he marries a local girl.
Maria Somethingopolis. Big name. Big family.

It won't last long, we said. And it didn't.
Took three of them, though. Stabbed him
in the back of a car, then set fire to it.

Cyprus One, England Nil. Mainly, though,
I remember the good times. Sound mates,
cheap bevvy. Moonlight on the Med. End of story.

No Surprises

He wakes when the sun rises
Gets up Exercises
Breakfasts with one whom he despises
Chooses one of his disguises
and his gun Fires his
first bullet It paralyses
Drives into town Terrorizes
Armed police in visors
materialize His demise is
swift No surprises.

Six Shooters

1

You are his repartee.
His last word on the subject.

After each row
he storms upstairs
and takes you out of
the dressingtable drawer.

He points you
at the bedroom door
and waits for her
to dare one final taunt.

'Come on up,' you croon.
'Come on up.'

2

She brazens it out.
Denies. Tries
to cover up
in a negligee of lies.

You, the lead hyphen
in between.
Infiltrator.

He loves her still
but she gone done him wrong.
You burst into song.

In a flash, all is forgiven.

3

Went through a war together
never left his side.

Back home, though illicit,
still his pride.

4 a.m. in the den now.
The note written. Suicide.

You don't care who
you kill do you?
With whom you fellate

Into whose mouth
you hurl abuse,
whose brains you gurgitate.

4

After the outlaw
has bitten the dust
(Never again to rise)

The sheriff
takes you for a spin
round his finger

then blows the smoke
from your eyes.

5

You rarely get the blame.
Always the man
behind the hand
that holds you

Always the finger
in front of the trigger
you squeeze.

You rarely get the blame.
Always the fool
who thinks that you're
the answer

Always the tool
who does just as
you please.

6

oiled
and snug
in a
moist
holster

six
deadly pearls
in a
gross
oyster

Greek Tragedy

Approaching midnight and the mezze unfinished
we linger over Greek coffee and consider
calling for the bill, when suddenly the door
bangs open, and out of the neon-starry sky

falls a dazed giant. He stumbles in
and pinballs his way between the tables
nicking ringlets of deep-fried calamari en route.
Nikos appears from the kitchen, nervous but soothing.

'Double moussaka,' grunts the giant,
'and two bottles of that retsina muck.'
He gazes around the taverna, now freeze-framed.
No tables are empty, but none are full.

You could have broken bits off the silence
and dipped them into your taramasalata.
Then he sees me. I turn to a rubberplant
in the far corner and try to catch its eye,

'Excuse me, can I have the bill, please?'
He staggers over and sits down. The chair groans
and the table shudders. 'I know you, don't I?'
he says. '"Lily the Pink" an' all that crap.

'Give us yer autograph. It's not for me,
it's for me nephew. Stick it on this.'
I sign the crumpled napkin as if it were
the Magna Carta and hand it back.

Then to my girlfriend I say overcheerfully,
'Time we were off, love.' While peering
at the napkin as if I'd blown my nose into it
he threatens: 'Youse are not goin' nowhere.'

On cue, a plate of cheesy mince and two bottles
appear. Flicking our hands from the top of the glasses
he refills them and looks at me hard. Very hard.
'D'ye know who I am?' (I do, but pretend I don't.)

'Eddie Mason. Call me Eddie.' 'Cheers, Eddie.'
'D'ye know what I do?' (I do, but pretend I don't.)
'I'm a villain. Livin' on the edge. Bit like you,
Know what I mean?' (I don't, but pretend I do.)

'I'm in the people business like yourself.'
Lest I am a doubting Thomas, he grabs my hand
and shoves a finger into a dent in his skull.
'Pickaxe. And feel tha' . . . and tha' . . . and tha'.'

Brick, hammer, knife, screwdriver, baseball bat.
He takes me on a guided tour of his scalp.
A map of clubs and pubs, doorways and dives.
Of scores settled and wounds not yet healed.

What he couldn't show me were the two holes
above the left eye, where the bullets went in
a fortnight later. Shot dead in the back of a cab
by the father of a guy whose legs he'd smashed

with an iron bar. He hardly touched
his moussaka, but he ordered more wine.
And it goes without saying, that he shredded
the napkin, and left without paying.

The Terrible Outside

The bus I often took as a boy to visit an aunt
went past it. From the top deck I would look
beyond the wall for signs of life: a rooftop protest,
a banner hung from cell windows. I would picture
the escape. Two men sliding down the rope
and legging it up Walton Vale. Maybe hijacking
the bus and holding us hostage. But I'd talk them
round. Share my sweets and pay their fares.

Years later I am invited there to run a poetry
workshop. An escapism easily contained.
And as I check in and pass through security,
and as door after door clangs open and shut,
I imagine that I am a prisoner. 'But I'm innocent,
I tell you. I was framed.' It's no use protesting,
take the old lag's advice, just keep your head down
and get on with it. The three hours will soon pass.

A class of eighteen. All lifers in their early twenties,
most with tattoos, childishly scratched and inked in.
Nervous, I remove my raincoat and shake my
umbrella. 'It's terrible outside,' I say. Then panic.
'I mean, compared to life inside it's not terrible . . .
It's good. It was the weather I was talking about.
Outside, it's really bad. But not as bad as in here,
of course. Being locked up . . . it must be terrible.'

They look at me blankly, wondering perhaps
if that was my first poem and not thinking much of it.
We talk. I read my stuff and they read theirs.
I answer questions (about fashion and music).
The questions I want to ask I can't. 'Hands up
those who killed their fathers? Hands up
those who killed more than once? Hands up . . .'
But those hands are clean, those faces bright.
Any one of them I'd trust with my life.

Or would I? Time's up and the door clangs open.
They all gather round and insist on shaking my hand.
A hand that touches women, that lifts pints, a hand
that counts money, that buttons up brand-new shirts.
A hand that shakes the hand of the Governor,
that raises an umbrella and waves down a cab.
A hand that trembles and clenches and pushes
itself deep into a raincoat pocket. A hand
that is glad to be part of the terrible outside.

The End of Summer

It is the end of summer
The end of day and cool,
As children, holiday-sated,
Idle happily home from school.

Dusk is slow to gather
The pavements still are bright,
It is the end of summer
And a bag of dynamite

Is pushed behind the counter
Of a department store, and soon
A trembling hand will put an end
To an English afternoon.

The sun on rooftops gleaming
Underlines the need to kill,
It is the end of summer
And all is cool, and still.

A Brown Paper Carrierbag

IN THE TIME . . .
    a spider's web woven across
    the plateglass window shivers snaps
    and sends a shimmering haze of lethal stars
    across the crowded restaurant

IN THE TIME IT TAKES . . .
    jigsaw pieces of shrapnel
    glide gently towards children
    tucking in   to the warm flesh
    a terrible hunger sated

IN THE TIME IT TAKES TO PUT DOWN . . .
    on the pavement
    people come apart   slowly
    at first
    only the dead not screaming

IN THE TIME IT TAKES TO PUT DOWN
A BROWN PAPER CARRIERBAG.

The Identification

So you think it's Stephen?
Then I'd best make sure
Be on the safe side as it were.
Ah, theres been a mistake. The hair

you see, its black, now Stephens fair . . .
Whats that? The explosion?
Of course, burnt black. Silly of me.
I should have known. Then lets get on.

The face, is that the face I ask?
that mask of charred wood
blistered, scarred could
that have been a child's face?
The sweater, where intact, looks
in fact all too familiar.
But one must be sure.

The scoutbelt. Yes thats his.
I recognise the studs he hammered in
not a week ago. At the age
when boys get clothes-conscious
now you know. Its almost
certainly Stephen. But one must
be sure. Remove all trace of doubt.
Pull out every splinter of hope.

Pockets. Empty the pockets.
Handkerchief? Could be any schoolboy's.
Dirty enough. Cigarettes?
Oh this can't be Stephen.
I dont allow him to smoke you see.
He wouldn't disobey me. Not his father.
But thats his penknife. Thats his alright.
And thats his key on the keyring
Gran gave him just the other night.
Then this must be him.

I think I know what happened
.   .   .   .   .   .   about the cigarettes
No doubt he was minding them
for one of the older boys.
Yes thats it.
Thats him.
Thats our Stephen.

A Cautionary Calendar

Beware January,
His greeting is a grey chill.
Dark stranger. First in at the kill.
Get out while you can.

Beware February,
Jolly snowman. But beneath the snow
A grinning skeleton, a scarecrow.
Don't be drawn into that web.

Beware March,
Mad Piper in a many-coloured coat
Who will play a jig then rip your throat.
If you leave home, don't go far.

Beware April,
Who sucks eggs and tramples nests.
From the wind that molests
There is no escape.

Beware May,
Darling scalpel, gall and wormwood.
Scented blossom hides the smell
Of blood. Keep away.

Beware June,
Black lipstick, bruise-coloured rouge,
Sirensong and subterfuge.
The wide-eyed crazed hypnotic moon.

Beware July,
Its juices overflow. Lover of excess
Overripe in flyblown dress.
Insatiable and cruel.

Beware August,
The finger that will scorch and blind
Also beckons. The only place you will find
To cool off is the morgue.

Beware September,
Who speaks softly with honeyed breath.
You promise fruitfulness. But death
Is the only gift that she'll accept.

Beware October,
Whose scythe is keenest. The old crone
Makes the earth tremble and moan.
She's mean and won't be mocked.

Beware November,
Whose teeth are sharpened on cemetery stones,
Who will trip you up and crunch your bones.
Iron fist in iron glove.

Beware December,
False beard that hides a sneer.
Child-hater. In what year
Will we know peace?

Kyrie

There was a porter
who had ideas
high above his railway station
always causing righteous indignation

he wanted to be
giant amongst men
saviour come again to earth
but his teachings only met with mirth

one bright winters morn
packed in his job
believed the world needed him
dedicated his life to fighting sin

the second day out
crossing the road
apparently in Stockport town
a diesel lorry swerved and knocked him down

back at the station
all the porters
wore mourning masks on their faces
and all agreed he should have stuck to cases

Train Crash

i once met a man
who had been in that crash
near Potters Bar

he said the worst thing
was the pause after
and the pause before

the bloody screaming
which though nervesplintttering
might well be heard

most nights on TV.
He spoke slowly
pausing   between   each   word

Funny sort of bloke

Have you heard the latest scandal
About 80-year-old Mr Brown?
He stole from Matron's handbag
Then hitchhiked into town.

Had a slap-up meal at the Wimpy
Then went to a film matinée
One of them sexy blue ones
We're not supposed to see.

Then he bought some jeans and a toupee
Spent the night in a pub
Then carried on till the early hours
Dancing in a club.

They caught him in the morning
Trying to board the London train
He tried to fight them off
But he's back here once again.

They asked him if he'd be a good boy
He said he'd rather not
So they gave him a nice injection
And tied him up in his cot.

He died that very night
Apparently a stroke.
Kept screaming: 'Come out Death and fight.'
Funny sort of bloke.

Uncle Harry

Uncle Harry was a widower
wouldn't have it another way
wore two pairs of socks all year round
with a prayer started each day:

> 'Oh God, let it be a coronary
> something quick and clean
> I've always been fastidious
> and death can be obscene.
>
> So if today You've put me down
> then it's Your will and I'm not scared
> but could it be at home please
> not where I'll look absurd,
>
> like on the street, at the match,
> in the toilet on a train
> (and preferably a one off
> in the heart and not the brain)'

Uncle Harry was a vegetarian
until the other day
collapsed on his way to the Health Food Store,
rushed to hospital, died on the way.

Good Old William

'I concur
with everything you say,'
smiled William.

'Oh yes,
I concur with that,
I agree.'

'If that's the general feeling
You can count on me.
Can't say fairer.'

Good old
William, the Concurrer.

Tide and time

My Aunty Jean
was no mean hortihorologist.
For my fifteenth birthday
she gave me a floral wristwatch.
Wormproof and self-weeding,
its tick was as soft
as a butterfly on tiptoe.

All summer long
I sniffed happily the passing hours.
Until late September
when, forgetting to take it off
before bathing at New Brighton,
the tide washed time away.

In Transit

She spends her life
in Departure Lounges,
flying from one to another.

Although planes frighten her,
baggage is a bother
and foreigners a bore,

in the stifled hysteria
of an airport
she, in transit, feels secure.

Enjoys the waiting game.
Cheered by storms, strikes
and news of long delays,

among strangers, nervous
and impatient for the off,
the old lady scrambles her days.

War of the Roses

Friday came the news.
Her G.P. rang and told her.
The telephone buckled
in her hand. Safely distanced,
he offered to come round.
'Why bother,' she said, 'Bastard.'

She had guessed anyway. The body
had been telling her for months.
Sending haemorrhages, eerie messages
of bruises. Outward signs
of inner turmoil. You can't sweep
blood under the carpet.

Thirty, single, living with and for
a four-year-old daughter. Smokes,
drinks whisky, works in television.
Wakes around four each morning
fearful and crying. Listens to
the rioting in her veins.

Her blood is at war with itself.
With each campaign more pain,
a War of the Roses over again.
She is a battlefield. In her,
Red and White armies compete.
She is a pair of crossed swords
on the medical map of her street.

What My Lady Did

I asked my lady what she did
   She gave me a silver flute and smiled.
A musician I guessed, yes that would explain
   Her temperament so wild.

I asked my lady what she did
   She gave me a comb inlaid with pearl.
A hairdresser I guessed, yes that would explain
   Each soft and billowing curl.

I asked my lady what she did
   She gave me a skein of wool and left.
A weaver I guessed, yes that would explain
   Her fingers long and deft.

I asked my lady what she did
   She gave me a slipper trimmed with lace.
A dancer I guessed, yes that would explain
   Her suppleness and grace.

I asked my lady what she did
　　She gave me a picture not yet dry.
A painter I guessed, yes that would explain
　　The steadiness of her eye.

I asked my lady what she did
　　She gave me a fountain pen of gold.
A poet I guessed, yes that would explain
　　The strange stories that she told.

I asked my lady what she did
　　She told me – and oh, the grief!
I should have guessed, she's under arrest
　　My lady was a thief!

W.P.C. Marjorie Cox

W.P.C. Marjorie Cox
brave as a lion
bright as an ox
is above all else, a girl.
Large of bosom
soft of curl.

Keeps in her dainty vanity case
diamanté handcuffs, trimmed with lace,
a golden whistle, a silken hanky,
a photograph of Reg Bosanquet
(signed: 'To Marjorie, with love'),
a truncheon in a velvet glove.

W.P.C. Marjorie Cox
cute as a panda
in bobby sox.
Men queue to loiter with intent
for the pleasure of an hour spent
in her sweet custody.

Poem for a Lady Wrestler

There be none of Beauty's daughters
 who can wrestle like thee
And like depth-charges on the waters
 is thy sweet voice to me.

Thy muscles are like tender alps
 with strength beyond compare
Of all the Ladies of the Rings
 there is none so fair.

Thy half-nelsons and thy head-locks
 thy slammings to the floor
are bliss. But in bedsocks
 and pyjamas I love thee even more.

Who Can Remember
Emily Frying?

The Grand Old Duke of Wellington
Gave us the wellington boot.
The Earl of Sandwich, so they say,
Invented the sandwich. The suit

Blues saxophonists choose to wear
Is called after Zoot Sims (a Zoot suit).
And the inventor of the saxophone?
Mr Sax, of course. (Toot! Toot!)

And we all recall, no trouble at all,
That buccaneer, long since gone,
Famed for his one-legged underpants –
'Why, shiver me timbers' – Long John.

But who can remember Emily Frying?
(Forgotten, not being a man.)
For she it was who invented
The household frying pan.

And what about Hilary Teapot?
And her cousin, Charlotte Garden-Hose?
Who invented things to go inside birdcages
(You know, for budgies to swing on). Those.

The Host

He can sing and dance
Play piano, trumpet and guitar.
An amateur hypnotist
A passable ventriloquist
Can even walk a tightrope
(But not far). When contracted,
Can lend a hand to sleight-of
And juggling. Has never acted,
But is, none the less, a Star.

He has a young wife. His third.
(Ex-au pair and former
Swedish Beauty Queen)
And an ideal home
In the ideal home counties.
His friends are household
Names of stage and screen,
And his hobbies are golf,
And helping children of those
Less fortunate than himself
Get to the seaside.

Having been born again. And again.
He believes in God. And God
Certainly believes in him.
Each night before going to bed
He kneels in his den
And says a little prayer:
'Thank you Lord, for my work and play,
Please help me make it in the U.S.A.'

Then still kneeling, with head bowed,
He tries out new material
(Cleaned up, but only slightly).
And the Almighty laughs out loud
Especially at jokes about rabbis
And the Pope. Just one encore
Then time for beddy-byes.
So he stands, and he bows,
Blows a kiss to his Saviour,
Then dances upstairs to divide Scandinavia.

The Tallest Man in Britain

I was in a room with the tallest man in Britain
And of one thing I could be certain
In no other room in Britain was there a man taller.

He agreed when I pointed out how tall he was.
'And I bet people say that to you all the time.'
He smiled wearily. 'No, as a matter of fact you're the first.'

To get into the *Guinness Book of Records*
All he had to do was get out of bed one morning
And measure himself.

Easier than sitting in a bathtub with 35 rattlesnakes
Easier than holding 109 venomous bees in your mouth
Easier than balancing a motorbike on your teeth for 14.5 seconds
Easier than riding a lawnmower across the USA in 42 days
Easier than roller blading blindfold across the Sahara. Backwards

'Wouldn't you rather be the *strongest* man in Britain?' I asked.
'Or the *fastest*? Or the *richest*?'
'No,' he said, 'I'm perfectly happy the way I am.'
And excusing himself, went off in search
Of somebody else to look down on.

Laughing, all the way to Bank

The beautiful girl
in the flowing white dress
struggled along the platform
at the Angel.

In one hand
she carried a large suitcase.
In the other, another.

On reaching me
she stopped. Green eyes flashing
like stolen butterflies.

'Would you be so kind
as to carry one for me,'
she asked, 'as far as Bank?'

I laughed: 'My pleasure.'
And it was. Safe from harm,
All the way to Bank,
Moist in my palm, one green eye.

Valentine

If I were a boat I'd steer to you
    A pair of tights, adhere to you

If I were a plumber I'd plumb your depths
    A pancake maker, I'd stuff your crepes

If I were a painter I'd paint you in oils
    A Bengal Lancer, I'd lance your boils

If I were thunder I'd clap you
    A long-distance runner, I'd lap you

If I were a breeze I'd ruffle your skirt
    A squeezy bottle, I'd give you a squirt

If I were a Big Dipper I'd go off your rails
    A wicket-keeper, I'd whip off your bails

If I were a wok I'd stir-fry you
    A Guardian Angel, be there by you

If I were a glass-blower I'd blow you a kiss
    If I were a poem, I'd end up like this.

As Every Bandage Dreams

As every bandage dreams
of being the Shroud of Turin
So do I dream
of enfolding you

As every aria longs
for Pavarotti's velvet tongue
So my body yearns
to interpret you

As every avalanche schemes
the ascent of Everest
So I aspire
to the view from your summit

As every oilslick licks its lips
at the thought of the Galapagos
So I long to stick around
and pound your beaches

As everything that is without feeling
Comes to life when put next to you
So do I.

Romantic

I'm a romantic.
I often want to bring you flowers
Leave notes under the pillow.
Billets doux. Fivers.

I'm a romantic.
Many's the time I've nearly bought
the unexpected gift.
Chocolates. Diamonds.

I'm a romantic.
How often do I think
of surprising you at the sink.
Pulling the wool over your eyes.

I'm a romantic.
Love on the lino: soapy chocolates,
Diamonds, crushed flowers, fivers,
Billets doux. Wool.

(Little packet, two-thirds full.)

Your Favourite Hat

Believe me when I tell you that
I long to be your favourite hat

The velvet one. Purply-black
With ribbons trailing at the back

The one you wear to parties, plays,
Assignations on red-letter days

Like a bat in your unlit hall
I'd hang until there came the call

To freedom. To hug your crown
As you set off through Camden Town

To run my fingers through your hair
Unbeknown in Chalcot Square

To let them linger, let them trace
My shadow cast upon your face

Until, on reaching the appointed place
(The pulse at your temple, feel it race!)

Breathless, you whisper: 'At last, at last.'
And once inside, aside I'm cast

There to remain as tick ticks by
Nap rising at each moan and sigh

Ecstatic, curling at the brim
To watch you naked, there with him

Until, too soon, the afternoon gone
You retrieve me, push me on

Then take your leave (as ever, in haste)
Me eager to devour the taste

Of your hair. Your temples now on fire
My tongue, the hatband as you perspire

To savour the dampness of your skin
As you window-gaze. Looking in

But not seeing. Over Primrose Hill
You dawdle, relaxed now, until

Home Sweet Home, where, safely back
Sighing, you impale me on the rack

Is it in spite or because of that
I long to be your favourite hat?

Today is Not a Day for Adultery

Today is not a day for adultery.
The sky is a wet blanket
Being shaken in anger. Thunder
Rumbles through the streets
Like malicious gossip.

Take my advice: braving
The storm will not impress your lover
When you turn up at the house
In an anorak. Wellingtons,
Even coloured, seldom arouse.

Your umbrella will leave a tell-tale
Puddle in the hall. Another stain
To be explained away. Stay in,
Keep your mucus to yourself.
Today is not a day for sin.

Best pick up the phone and cancel.
Postpone until the weather clears.
No point in getting soaked through.
At your age, a fuck's not worth
The chance of catching 'flu.

Fits and Starts

His love life is one of fits and starts
      Claims he works as 'something in the City'
(partly true, he works at Marks & Sparks)

Engaged once to a student nurse at Bart's
      Who broke it off ('He's sad, a sort of Walter Mitty')
His love life is one of fits and starts

Twice a week he goes with dodgy tarts
    Half his wages on the nitty-gritty
(though not, it must be said, at Marks & Sparks)

Life can be the pits, and it's a pity
    To distil one little life into a ditty.
On your marks: his love life is one of
    Fits and starts – If it fits, it starts.

The Map

Wandering lost and lonely in Bologna
I found a street-map on the piazza.
Unfortunately, it was of Verona.

As I was refolding it into a limp concertina,
A voice: 'Ah, you've found it! I'm Fiona,
Let me buy you a spritzer, over there on the terrazza.'

Two spritzers later we ordered some pasta
(Bolognese, of course, then zabaglione).
I felt no remorse, merely amore.

Proposing a toast to love at first sight
We laughed and talked over a carafe of chianti
When out of the night, like a ghost, walked my aunty.

'Look who's here,' she cried. 'If it isn't our Tony,
Fancy bumping into you in Italy,
With a lady friend too,' then added, bitterly:

'How are Lynda and the kids? I'm sure they're OK.
While the mice are at home the tomcat will play.'
A nod to Fiona, 'Nice to meet you. Ciao!'

I snapped my grissini. 'Stupid old cow!'
Then turned to Fiona. She was no longer there.
Our romance in tatters, like the map on her chair.

Whoops!

You are strangely excited
as we enter the crowded bar
and find a small table in the corner.

You insist on fetching the drinks
and before disappearing
squeeze a note into my hand.

It reads: 'Why go home tonight?
I have a room. I have a bed.
I have a spare toothbrush.'

I recognize my own handwriting.

Dialectically Opposed

In Bristol, to escape the drizzle
One November afternoon, I ventured
Into a large book shop, George's,
Opposite the university where I was
To read that same evening.

It was my custom in those days
To sniff out my slim volumes
And give them due prominence.
Covers outfacing, three or four titles
Would see off most of the opposition.

But on this occasion, try as I might
(and I might have tried harder),
I could find no poetry whatsoever.
Then I spotted the Information Desk
Behind which was a girl with large bristols.

(I mention this, not to be sexist
But to remind you of that fair city.)
'Excuse me,' I said. 'Do you have
a Poetry Section?' Rose-Marie replied:
'I think you'll find it under Livestock.'

I stood, quandried to the spot.
'Livestock? Poetry? Books of Verse?'
The penny dropped. I watched its descent
Into the perfumed gorge of Avon.
'Poeltry,' she laughed. 'I thought you said Poultry!'

Bath – Avon

I have a problem with Bath.
I use the short *a*, rhyming it with *math*,
Whereas southerners put in the *r. Barth.*

So my living there would be a kind of hell
(Although a lovely place by all accounts).
Never have an operation you cannot spell
Or live in a town you mispronounce.

The Examination

'Well doctor, what do you think?'
He took the poem and examined it.
'Mmmm . . .'
The clock ticked nervously.
'This will have to come out for a start.'
He stabbed a cold finger into its heart.
'Needs cutting here as well.
This can go.
And this is weak. Needs building up.'
He paused . . .
'But it's the Caesura I'm afraid,

Can't do much about that.'
My palms sweated.
'Throw it away and start again, that's my advice.
And on the way out, send in the next patient, will you?'

I buttoned up my manuscript and left.
Outside, it was raining odes and stanzas.
I caught a crowded anthology and went directly home.

Realizing finally that I would never be published.
That I was to remain one of the alltime great unknown poets,
My work rejected by even the vanity presses,
I decided to end it all.

Taking an overdose of Lyricism
I awaited the final peace
When into the room burst the Verse Squad
Followed by the Poetry Police.

The Poet Takes an Autumnal Stroll on Hampstead Heath

Light rain, like steam
from a cup of camomile tea
poured from a copper kettle
heated o'er a sandalwood fire
bids him return home
and consider an alternative career.

Creative Writing

Why can't I teach Creative Writing in Minnesota?
Or, better still, be Poet in Residence in Santa Fe?
Where golden-limbed girls with a full quota
Of perfect teeth lionize me, feed me, lead me astray.

A professorship, perhaps, visiting in Ann Arbor?
(Nothing too strenuous, the occasional social call.)
What postcards I can write, what ambitions I can harbour:
Hawaii in the springtime, Harvard in the fall.

Meeting the Poet at Victoria Station

A day off for you to recover from jetlag
and then the tour begins in Brighton.
Neither met nor talked, but I like your poems
and the face on the back of your Selected.

No sign of you under the station clock
nor at the ticket office, so I make my way
to platform 12. Do I hear castanets?
Tap dancers busking for the pure fun of it?

No. Sitting on the floor, back to the wall
surrounded by bags, books and foolscap,
a woman is pounding a typewriter, oblivious
of commuters stepping around and over her.

You are dressed all in black, wearing glasses,
and your hair is wilder than in the photograph.
Not too late for me to turn back and ring
the Arts Council: 'Laryngitis' . . . 'Gingivitis' . . . 'St Vitus'

Instead, I ask you to dance. You give me your hand
and I whisk you across the marble floor,
my arm around your waist in the old-fashioned way.
Waltz, Foxtrot, Villanelle, Quickstep.

Ticket inspectors clear the way for us
as I guide you in and out of Knickerbox.
Shoppers stop and applaud as we twirl
around the shelves of W. H. Smith and Boots.

A Tango so erotic that Victoria blushes.
Rush hour but nobody is going anywhere
except in a centipedic circle as we lead
the customers in a Conga round the concourse.

A voice over the tannoy: 'Take your partners . . .'
Rumba, Samba, Salsa, Sestina.
Things are hotting up as the tempo quickens
Charleston, Terza Rima, Cha Cha Cha.

Suddenly the music stops.
'Excuse me,' I say, 'are you the poet?'
Removing her glasses she looks up from the typewriter.
'How did you guess?' I help carry her bags to the train.

Blazing fruit
(or The Role of the Poet as Entertainer)

During dinner the table caught fire.
No one alluded to the fact
and we ate on, regardless of
the flames singeing our conversation.

Unaware of the smoke
and the butlers swooning,
topics ranged from Auden
to Zeffirelli. I was losing
concentration however, and being
short on etiquette, became tense
and began to fidget with the melting cutlery.

I was fashioning a spoon
into a question mark
when the Chablis began to steam
and bubble. I stood up,
mumbled something about having left the gas running
and fled blushing
across the plush terrain of the carpet.

The tut-tut-tutting could be heard above
the cra-cra-cracking of the bone china.

Outside, I caught a cab
to the nearest bus stop.
While, back at the table,
they were toying with blazing fruit
and discussing the Role of the Poet as Entertainer,
when the roof fell in.

Take a poem, Miss Smith

'Take a poem, Miss Smith.
I will call it *The Ploughman*.
"The ploughman wearily follows the plough,
The dust that lies upon his brow,
Gnarled as the dead oak tree bough,
Makes me think of how . . . of how . . ."
How nice you smell, Miss Smith.
Is it Chanel? I thought so.
But to work: "The ploughman wearily follows . . ."
Ah, but I am wearied of ploughing.
File it away under "Nature – unfinished".

'Take a poem, Miss Smith.
It is entitled *Belfast*.
"Along the Shankhill Road, a pall
Of smoke hangs, thick as . . . thick as . . ."
Hair, something different about the hair.
A new style? It suits you.
But where was I? Oh yes:
"Along the Shankhill Road . . ."
No, I feel unpolitical today.
Put it away in the file
marked "Wars – unfinished".

'Take a poem, Miss Smith.
It will be known as *Flesh*.
"The flesh I love to touch
Is soft as . . . soft as . . ."
Take off your blouse, Miss Smith,
I feel a love poem coming on . . .'

An Ordinary Poetry Reading

Tonight will be an ordinary poetry reading
A run-of-the-mill kind of affair
Nothing that will offend or challenge
No *language* as far as I'm aware.

The poets are thoroughly decent
All vetted by our committee
We had hoped Wendy Cope might appear
But she's tied up more's the pity.

And that other one, whose name I forget . . .
Quite famous . . . Recently died . . .
He'd have been good. But never mind,
At least we can say that we tried.

Personally, I prefer actors
Reading the Great Works of the Past
The trouble with poets is they mumble
Get nervous, and then speaktoofast.

And alcohol is a danger
So that's been kept well out of sight
As long as they're sober this evening
They can drink themselves legless all night.

By the way, they've come armed with slim volumes
Which of course, they're desperate to sell
Otherwise, there's coffee in the foyer
With KitKats and Hobnobs as well.

Well, I think that covers everything
All that remains for me to say
Is to wish you . . . an ordinary evening
Such a pity I'm unable to stay.

After the Reading

'Where do you get your ideas from?'
said the lady in fur coat and trainers,
holding out a book for me to sign.

'Do you mind if I sit down, I'm all of a tizzy?
You must excuse me, I haven't been myself
since it happened. Three weeks ago and I'm still shaking.

I was walking down the road minding nobody's
business but my own, when, suddenly,
it leaped out at me. There was no escape.

My back to the railings. Straight out of Hitchcock
it was. A nightmare. I fought to protect myself
from this mad thing that was going for my throat.

Then a man's voice cried out, "Get in. Get in."
He'd pulled up and was holding the car door open.
But before I could close it after me the dog leaped in.

It went for his face. There was blood everywhere.
And the screaming. People on the pavement screaming.
Straight out of Hitchcock it was. Blood and screaming.

That's why I'm like this now, you see. I can't relax.
Three weeks ago and the police haven't done nothing.
More concerned about the dog than me. I rang up.

"It belonged to a farmer," they said, "but it's fine now."
"So bloody what," I said, "but what about me?"
"That's a civil matter," they said, "not criminal."

"Criminal? It's bloody surreal." I was standing there
bandaged up to my elbow, drugged up to the eyeballs,
cradling the telephone like a baby. "What about me?"

"Don't worry," said the policeman, "the dog's fine.
As a matter of fact, he's lying here in front of me
on the lino eating a sheep's head. Happy as Larry."

I couldn't believe my ears. Who's mad? I thought
to myself. Who's mad?' She gave me back the book.
'Would you mind putting the date on as well, please?'

Clone

A genetic scientist
With literary leanings
Cloned old verses
And gave them new meanings

A genetic scientist
With literary leanings
Cloned old verses
And gave them new meanings

A genetic scientist
With literary leanings
Cloned old verses
And gave them new meanings

Muffin the Cat
Written at the Arvon Foundation, Lumb Bank, Yorkshire

I had never considered cats
until Nadia said I should:
'If a person likes a cat,
then that person must be nice.'
So I seized the chance to be good
by taking her advice.

When Muffin (not the mule) called
around midnight to inspect the room
I was, at first, distinctly cool.
Until, remembering the New Me,
I praised felinity and made tea.
Offered him a biscuit. A cigarette.
Tried to make conversation.
He'd not be drawn. Not beaten yet
I showed him my collection
of Yugoslavian beermats.
He was unimpressed. (Queer, cats.)

At 2 a.m. I got out the whisky.
He turned up his nose.
After a few glasses I told him
about the problems at home.
The job. My soul I laid bare.
And all he did was stare.
Curled up on the duvet
with that cat-like expression.
Not a nod of encouragement.
Not a mew. Imagine the scene;
I felt like that intruder
on the bed with the Queen.

But I soldiered on till morning
and despite his constant yawning
told him what was wrong with the country.
The class system, nuclear disarmament,
the unions, free-range eggs.
I don't know what time he left.
I fell asleep. Woke up at four
With a hangover the size of a Yorkshire Moor.
And my tongue (dare I say it?) furry.

Since then, whenever I see the damn thing
He's away up the mountain to hide.
And I was only being friendly.
I tried, Nadia, I tried.

The Logic of Meteors

August in Devon and all is rain. A soft rain
that seems, not to fall from the sky, but to rise
from the ground and drape itself over the trees
and hedgerows like a swirl of silver taffeta.
But I am not interested in matters meteorological.
Not for me the logic of meteors, but the logic of metre.
For this is a Poetry Course and I am the Tutor.

Last night I had a visitor. (Not a female student:
'I'm having trouble with my sestina' . . . 'Please come in . . .')
But a monster that kamikazied around the room
before ensnaring itself within the vellum lampshade.
Waiting until the moth, light-headed, went into free fall
I clumped it with Ted Hughes' *Birthday Letters*
bringing to an end its short and insubstantial life.

Consumed with guilt? Hardly. A frisson of imagined
Buddhism? Possibly. Would Mrs Moth and the kids
be at home waiting? Unlikely. It was either me or it.
For who is to say that my visitor wasn't a mutant killer
waiting for me to fall asleep before stuffing itself
down my throat and bringing to a suffocating end
this short and insubstantial life . . . Do I hear thunder?

*   *   *

A second meteor, a host-carrier bearing aliens from
the Planet of the Moths, tears a hole in the damp taffeta
at the hem of the hills surrounding Black Torrington.
A soft rain still, but high above, a vellum moon.
In his room, the Tutor pours himself a large scotch,
guiltily wipes the smear of blood from the dust-jacket
and settles down, unaware of the avenging, impending swarm.

His poems are nets

His poems are nets
in which he hopes
to capture girls

He makes them at work
or late at night
when pubs are closed

He uses materials
at hand. Scraps
of conversation, jokes,

lines lifted from
dead poets (he likes
a bit of poetry in his poems)

* * *

He washes his hair
for the reading
and wears tight pants

When it comes to him
he swaggers out
unzipping his file

Exposes small dreams
which he breaks
with a big stick

His verse a mag
nifying glass
held up to his prick

* * *

His poems are nets
and like nets
can be seen through

Girls bide their time
Wait for the singer
to throw them a line.

A Critic Reviews the Curate's Egg

'It's all bad.
Especially in parts.'

Two Riddles

(i)

To ease us
Through those difficult days

At hand to tease out
Waifs and strays

Though causing pain
We squeeze you again

And again. Vain? Not really
More a fear of the unruly

If you wish to borrow mine
Simply repeat the opening line.

(ii)

A rat (black) rattles across the floor
A cross (red) daubed upon the door.

A bell (muffled) rung in the early dawn
A grave (deep) dug far away from town.

A tumbril (full) trundles down the lane
Tomorrow (and tomorrow) it will trundle again.

People avoid me like the plague
What am I?

The Nearest Forty-two

I want to write a new poem.
What words shall I choose?
I go in. The variety is endless.
Images stretch into infinity.

I dither. Can't make up my mind.
Inspiration becomes impatient.
Stamps its feet. Panicking
I grab the nearest forty-two,

The Written Word
(a Full Monty of poetic forms)

A poet of little repute
    Desperate for something to do
One evening pissed as a newt
    Decided to have a tattoo.

On his chest an unrhymed sestina
    On his belly a fine villanelle
On each bicep a series of haiku
    On each shank a tanka as well.

On each shoulder a Petrarchan sonnet
    Making twenty-eight lines in all
An acrostic across each firm buttock
    With a limerick, what else? on each ball.

On each knee, though knobbly, a rondeau redoublé
    (which was terribly tricky to do)
On each pendulous lobe, a Pindaric ode
    On each clavicle, a neat clerihew.

Any flesh that remained was minutely quatrained
    (the odd couplet if not enough room)
On the sole of each foot, a virelai was put
    An englyn and Malaysian pantoum.

* * *

This poet of Great Repute
  Now travels from town to town
Goes on stage, removes his shirt
  And takes his trousers down.

While audiences marvel
  At the body of work so vast
Concrete, surreal and post-modern
  Alongside the great works of the past.

And some are poetry-lovers
  Who believe they could do worse
Than curl up every evening
  With this anthology of verse.

For nothing can beat the written word
Especially on a torso, bared.

Word Trap

Sometimes they trap me
Stop me in my tracks.

Thinking my way through
Towards a promising idea

When I am distracted
By a sound. A spelling crackles.

Without a second thought
I am off into the thicket.

The next thing I know
It is time for bed.

Another poem finished
And nothing said.

'I found I could not use the long line because of my
nervous nature.'

– William Carlos Williams

As soon as my voice is heard above the babble
Which ceases as people turn
I want to disappear. Hide under the table.

My pulse races and I consequently gabble.
Puzzled faces make mine burn
And make it crystal clear – I'm from Planet Babel.

On the Point of Extinction

Manx: The celtic dialect (Manx Gaelic) of the Isle of
Man, now on the point of extinction.

Pears Encyclopaedia, 78th edition

An old man walks into his local newsagents
and asks, in perfect Manx, for a packet of Silk Cut
and the *Daily Mirror* . . . Oh, and some aspirin
for the missus. The man behind the counter,
being new to the area, says, 'Pardon?'

Tobaccoless, paperless and aspirinless,
the old man returns home to find his wife
collapsed on the living-room floor.
He telephones immediately for an ambulance,
but the girl from the Emergency Services Provider,
being in Manchester, says, 'Pardon?'

The old man rushes out into the busy street
and in pure Manx Gaelic appeals for help
to the passers-by. They either nod sympathetically
and give directions to the ferry, or say, 'Pardon?'

The old woman dies. The old man is struck dumb.
And Manx Gaelic, having nobody to talk to,
sets off in search of the Land of Lost Tongues
as fast as his three legs can carry him.

The death of John Berryman in slow motion

We open on a frozen river
(the spot where the poet has arranged to meet death).
The whiteness is blinding.
The glare hurts our eyes.

From somewhere above he jumps.
We see the shadow first
seeping into the ice
like a bruise. Thickening.

There is no sound but the wind
skulking beneath the bridge.

Now the body comes into shot.
Falling, blurred, a ragged bearskin.
The shadow opens its arms to greet it.

The wind is holding its breath.

We freeze frame at the moment of impact
(noting the look of surprise on the poet's face).
We then pan slowly upwards
to the grey Minnesota sky.

Fade to black.

One Poet May Hide Another
(for Kenneth Koch)

Kenya
A car held up at a railroad crossing
At the wheel, the poet.
To pass the time he writes a poem.

London
Holed up in his study, a second poet
Reads the poem, then ducks.
He realizes that it may hide another.

However
He is unprepared for the train
That comes hurtling out of the fireplace
Followed by another, and another, and

A Visit to the Poet and his Wife
(for Sidney and Nessie Graham)

To set the scene: A cave
in Madron, Cornwall.
On a warm September afternoon
Mr and Mrs W.S.G. are 'at home'
to admirers bearing distilled gifts.

Mine host, after clearing
a mess of mss from the table
takes *implements in their places*
from its place, and puts on
spectacles to clear the air.

A warm, brown voice
with silver whiskers unveils
a poem that is the spitting
image of itself. The onlisteners
are amazed at its likeness.

Tumblers, half-filled with malt,
are topped up with bright
watery sunshine by the good
Lady of the Cottage. The afternoon
saddens at its own passing.

To set the scene: A cave
in Madron, Cornwall.
On a warm September afternoon
Mr and Mrs W.S.G. are 'at home'
to admirers bearing distilled gifts.

All for Laurie Lee
(written for his 80th birthday)

I love the way he uses words
Will they work the same for me?
'Sorry' said the words,
'We only do it for Laurie Lee'

But words are common property
They're available and free
Said the words: 'We're very choosy
And we've chosen Laurie Lee'

I want to write like he does
But the words did all agree:
'Sorry son we're spoken for,
We belong to Laurie Lee!'

Educating Rita
(for W.R.)

Come in and welcome. You're the first.
Let me take your things. Go straight through.
Now something to quench the nation's thirst?
There's lager by the crate. A nice Moselle

Local and highly recommended?
Or there's whisky, vodka, gin as well.
When everyone's arrived we'll serve champagne
And wet the baby's head.

God it's hot. Never thought I'd miss rain.
But there you go. The auld country?
Not as much as I thought I would.
Fresh strawberries. Spring perhaps. And Guinness
Which doesn't travel well and never should.
Susan misses it more I believe.
The way ex-Scousers talk about the place
You wonder why they leave:
'Ferries across the Mersey, the old Pier 'Ead,
Chip butties, the Kop, six in a bed,
The "gents" in the Phil, a cathedral to spare,
Liver birds with long fair hair.'
And going on and on about the native wit
You'd think the buggers had invented it.
But deep down she's no regrets I'm sure.
She needed new friends, a fresh challenge.
She's her own woman now, more mature.
She'll be down in a minute with the star of the show.

Oh by the way, the Russells are coming
Whom I think you all know.
Nice couple. Although Willy will insist
On playing guitar and singing when he's pissed.
And exciting news, I think you'll all agree,
There's a real live actress coming too
Who's starred in a West End theatre show.
Filming out here, just passing through.
So all you sheilas take real good care
Lest Bruce or Norm disappear from the parlour
Into the yard to show her a Koala bear.

No thanks, I've given up. Feel better for it.
Part of Susan's two-year plan for a new and fitter man.
She's even got me jogging. I adore it.

Yes she loves teaching. Can't wait to get back.
And to be honest, neither can I.
Need the money since I got the sack.
Mind you, things couldn't have worked out neater
Means I can spend all my time with the baby
Bringing up and educating Rita. Why Rita?
Just our little secret. A name that binds us.
And here they come now. The two I love the most.
Aren't I a lucky man? Ladies and Gentlemen – A toast!

This be Another Verse

They don't fuck you up, your mum and dad
(Despite what Larkin says)
It's other grown-ups, other kids
Who, in their various ways

Die. And their dying casts a shadow
Numbering all our days
And we try to keep from going mad
In multifarious ways.

And most of us succeed, thank God,
So if, to coin a phrase
You're fucked up, don't blame your mum and dad
(Despite what Larkin says).

The Darling Buds of Maybe
Get out as early as you can,
And don't have any kids yourself.

'Perfick,' said Old Larkin
The last kid put to bed
He took the Missus in his arms
Gave her a kiss and said:

'I'll pop out for a quick one
If that's all right with you?
I'll not be long, I promise
'Cos I've got work to do.'

'You mean the roof,' said Ma,
'You're going to mend that leak?'
Philip stopped.
'No, "This Be The Verse",
That final stanza's too bleak.'

From 'Les Pensées'
by Le Duc de Maxim

Beside the willowèd river bank
Repose I, still and thinking,
When into the water fall a man
Who fast begin the sinking.

Chance at last to test
A maxim, so unblinking,
I toss to him the straw
Through which I drinking.

Sure enough, he clutch the straw
And scream, alas in vain.
He grasp until he gasp his last
And all is peace again.

Homewardly I pensive trek
Impatient now to note
How the fingers of the sun
Did linger on his throat.

And how he sank, and how
The straw continuèd to float,
'How wise the age-old axioms,
And yet how sad,' I wrote.

Toffee

It gives me no pleasure to say this
But he won't be missed.
Resentful when sober, aggressive when pissed.

Though not proven, it is rumoured
That he pays to be spanked.
And worse, he can't write for toffee.

Small magazine stuff over the years.
The same poem thinly disguised.
Recycled, retitled, endlessly revised.

I would like to say that book launches
Will never be the same
Without his snide comments.

That literary gatherings will seem tame
Without his drunken outbursts.
But I can't.

It does me no credit to say this
But in his sad case,
Posthumous the better.

Poetspotting

On the train to Bangor from Crewe
Jo Shapcott and I, as tutors tend to do
gossip, and get to wonder

which of the passengers are headed
for Ty Newydd. That orange-haired
punk in tight leather? Unlikely.

More likely the old lady wearing purple
(see Jenny Joseph), daring people
to come close, if any do, they're kissed.

Or, pissed in the corner, surrounded
by throttled cans of Guinness,
the man who shakes a mottled first

at a muse unseen, and screams:
'Orange, orange, there must be
a rhyme for feckin' orange!'

Trust Me, I'm a Poet

Your husband upped and left you
After years of playing the field?
My heart goes out, I know the type
Of course, my lips are sealed.
Let me be your confidant
I'm generous, let me show it
Champagne, I think is called for
Trust me, I'm a poet.

*   *   *

Put my wallet on the counter
When I turned round it had gone
And I've got to meet my agent
In town, for lunch at one
To sign a five-book contract
I'll be back before you know it
Can you lend me fifty quid?
Trust me, I'm a poet.

Wheelchairs

After a poetry reading at a geriatric
hospital in Birmingham, December 1983

I go home by train
with a cig and a Carly.
Back at the gig
the punters, in bed early
dither between sleep and pain:
'Who were those people?
What were they talking?'

The staff,
thankful for the break,
the cultural intrusion,
wheel out the sherry
and pies. Look forward
to a merry Christmas
and another year of caring
without scrutiny.

Mutiny!
In a corner,
the wheelchairs,
vacated now, are cooling.
In the privacy of darkness
and drying piss,
sullen-backed,
alone at last,
they hiss.

For Want of a Better Title

The Countess
when the Count passed away

During a Bach
cello recital

Married an Archduke
the following day

For want of a better title.

Memento Mori

I still have the blue beret that JFK
was wearing the day he was assassinated.

If you take the nipple between finger and thumb,
hold it up to the light and twirl it round

you can see the bullet holes (or, to be precise,
the two holes made by a single bullet).

For many years I kept in store, the fox-fur stole
that Virginia Woolf wore in March 1941

when she walked into the River Ouse at Rodmell.
But those sharp, little eyes had seen too much.

They disturbed me so I disposed of it.
This leather jacket, however, I would not sell

for a million pounds. Her Royal Highness
was wearing it on that dreadful night in Paris

when her Harley-Davidson skidded on black ice.
This may interest you. John Berryman's silver

fob watch, still showing 9.24. The exact time
he hit the frozen river. Minneapolis, 1972.

A Serious Poem

This is a serious poem
It wears a serious face
It will not fritter away the words
It knows its place.

Perfectly balanced
Neither too long nor too short
It gazes solemnly heavenwards
Like a real poem ought.

Familiar with the classics
It drops names with ease.
Here comes Plato with Lycidas
And look, there's Demosthenes!

A serious poem will often end
With two lines that rhyme.
But not always.

Awful Acrobats

Poets make awful acrobats.
Good at barely moving
Idle musing has impaired
Their sense of balance.

Once the horizon tilts
Everything begins to slide:
Cups and saucers, trees,
Buildings, spirit-levels.

Out of touch with the ground
They are out of touch with themselves.
Struggling to make sense of air
They become entangled with it.

The roll of drums:
A few floppy cartwheels
A crumpled somersault
Then up on to the high wire . . .

After the first falter, the fall.
It is faultless. The safety-net
Holds out its arms. The poet

                                       misses.

(Gravity hangs its head in shame.)

*　　*　　*

Poets have a way with language
A certain jauntiness with hats

They can make a decent curry
And are very fond of cats

Though some are closet fascists
In the main they're democrats

But all things being considered
Poets make awful acrobats.

It's Only a P . . .

Feeling a trifle smug after breaking off an untidy,
Drawn-out affair with somebody I no longer fancied
I was strolling through Kensington Gardens
When who should I bump into but Gavin.

Gavin, I should point out, is the husband.
'I'm worried about Lucy,' he said, straight out.
'I don't blame you,' I thought, but said nothing.
'Suspect she's having an affair. Any ideas?'

'Divorce,' I suggested. 'You might even get custody.'
'No, I mean Lucy,' he persisted. 'Who with?'
We walked on in silence, until casually, I asked:
'An affair, you say, what makes you so convinced?'

He stopped and produced from an inside pocket
A sheet of paper which I recognized at once.
It was this poem. Handwritten, an early draft.
Then I saw the gun. 'For God's sake, Gavin,
                                    It's only a p . . .

It's Only a P . . . Part Two

A shot rang out. The bullet was not intended for me.
It embedded itself harmlessly into a tall sycamore.
(Harmlessly, that is, except for the tall sycamore.)
Gavin pocketed the gun. I was shaking like a leaf.

I seized his arm. 'It's over now,' I stammered
'There was nothing in it really. A moment of madness.'
I was lying and wondered if he could tell.
He gave no sign, so relaxing my grip we walked on.

'You'd better have this,' he said, and held out the poem.
'But I'd rather you didn't publish. Spare my blushes.'
I took it. 'If not for me for Lucy's sake.'
'Trust me,' I said and crumpled it into a ball.

Behind us, the sycamore rose swaying from the bushes,
Staggered across the ornamental lake
And collapsed against a wall.

Coach and Horses

One of those poems you write in a pub
on a wet Friday. On your own and nothing to read.
Surrounded by people hugging each other with language.

But you are not without a friend in the world.
You are not here simply for the Alc. 5.5% Vol.
To prove it, you appear to have had a sudden thought.

Writing, like skinning beermats, is displacement activity.
You word-doodle with crazed concentration,
feigning oblivion to the conversations that mill around.

The seductive, the leery, arm in arm with the slurred
and the weary. For some reason, possibly alcoholic,
the doodles coalesce into a train of thought.

Actively displaced, you race along the platform
as it gathers speed. But before you can jump aboard
Time is called, and it comes off the rails.

But this is your secret. Unacknowledged legislator,
you drink up and leave, with a poem so full of holes
you could drive a coach and horses through it.

Poem for a dead poet

He was a poet he was.
A proper poet.
He said things
that made you think
and said them nicely.
He saw things
that you or I
could never see
and saw them clearly.
He had a way
with language.
Images flocked around
him like birds,
St Francis, he was,
of the words. Words?
Why he could almost make 'em talk.

The Filmmaker
(with subtitles)

He was a filmmaker with a capital F.
Iconoclastic. He said 'Non' to Hollywood,   1
'Pourquoi? Ici je suis Le Chef.'   2
A director's director. Difficult but good.

But when Mademoiselle La Grande C.   3
Crept into his bed in Montparnasse
And kissed him on the rectum, he
Had a rectumectomy. But in vain. Hélas.   4

And how they mourned, the aficionados.
(Even stars he'd not met were seen to grieve,
The Christies, Fondas, Streeps and Bardots.)
And for them all, he'd one last trick up his sleeve.

'Cimetière Vérité' he called it (a final pun).   5
In a fashionable graveyard in Paris 3ième.
He was buried, and at the going down of the sun
Premiered his masterpiece, *La Mort, C'est Moi-même.*   6

The coffin, an oblong, lead-lined studio with space
For the body, a camera and enough light
To film in close-up that once sanguine face
Which fills the monumental screen each night.

The show is 'Un grand succès'. People never tire   7
Of filing past. And in reverential tone
They discuss the symbolism, and admire
Its honesty. *La Vérité* pared down to the bone.   8

FIN   9

1 'No.'   2 'Why? Here I am the chef.'   3 Miss the Big C.
4 Alas.   5 'True cemetery'.   6 *The Death it is Myself.*
7 'A grand success'.   8 The Truth.   9 End.

When I Am Dead

I could never begin a poem: 'When I am dead'
As several poets still alive have done.
The jokey Last Will, and litanies
Of things we are to do when they have gone.

Courageous stuff. Written I shouldn't wonder
The Morning After, in the throes
Of grim despair. Head still ringing from the noise
Of nights keeling over like glass dominoes.

The chill fear that perhaps the writer
Might outlive the verse, provides the spur
To nail the spectre down in print,
To risk a sort of atheistic prayer.

God, of course, does not appear in rhyme,
Poets of our time being more inclined
To dwell upon the price of manuscripts
And how they want the coffin lined.

Or ashes scattered, cats fed, ex-wives
Gunned down. Meanwhile, in a drawer
Neat and tidy, the bona fide Will,
Drawn-up and witnessed by an old family lawyer.

And though poets I admire have published poems
Whose imperfections reflect our own decay,
I could never begin a poem: 'When I am dead'
In case it tempted Fate, and Fate gave way.

Repelled by Metal

I don't drive, I'm afraid.
Never had the inclination or the need.
Being antimagnetic, I am repelled by metal
And unimpressed by speed.

Nor am I being 'holier than thou'.
Thou art a godsend to be candid
You with the car and the welcoming smile
Without your lift I'd be stranded.

And it's not that I dislike cars
Though noisy and dangerous I dare say
Money-eaters and poison-excreters, okay
But I don't dislike cars, per se.

It's just that I know my limitations.
I'd be all thumbs behind a wheel.
Don't laugh. Could you park a poem
In a space this small? Well, that's how I feel.

The Oxford Book of Twentieth-Century English Verse
(Reviewed by Georges Perec)

This havy volum is a must for popl who lik potry.
Pom aftr pom, in a glorious fast of litratur.
Mmorabl simils and mtaphors ar vrywhr
whil fin rhyms and imags lap out from vry pag.

Grat poms ar faturd from th liks of Louis MacNic,
John Btjman, Hilair Blloc, T. S. Liot and Td Hughs.
Not forgtting Larkin's favorit pot, Hardy, who has
twnty svn poms comprd to only nin by W. B. Yats.

This anthology, though havily criticzd by thos pots
who ar not includd, is likly to rmain a standard
work for many yars. My only quibbl is that Frnch
pots ar xcludd for rasons known only to th ditor.

French novelist, the late Georges Perec, published a 50,000-word novel,
La Disparition (1969), entirely omitting the letter 'e'.

I Don't Like the Poems

I don't like the poems they're making me write
I really don't like them at all
Hierograffiti I don't understand
Scrawled on a hologrammed wall.

They wake me up in the middle of the night
I really don't like them one bit
Dictating mysterious messages
That I am forced to transmit.

Messages with strange metaphors, ass-
onance, similes and the like.
Internal rhymes that chime, and alas
External ones that sometimes don't quite make it.

I don't like the poems they filter through me
Using words I never would use
Like 'filter', 'hierograffiti', 'alien'
I'm enslaved by an alien muse.

*   *   *

And I notice, just lately, at readings
That friends whose work I have known
Unknowingly have started to write
In a similarly haunted tone.
Stumbling over poems we have to recite
In handwriting that isn't our own.

Porno Poem

I felt dirty having to write this poem
But an obscene amount of cash was on offer
And had I refused you can be sure
That another poet would have rushed in.
As the reader of course, you are under
No obligation to get involved. Feel free to go.

(Cue music)
A woman with no clothes on is lying on a bed.
A man with no clothes on enters the bedroom.
They do sex. *(Cue FX sighs, groans, etc.)*

There. That's the porno done and dusted
And to be honest, I'm glad that it's over.
However, as you chose to read on
Perhaps you now regret having taken part
In the whole sordid affair. Especially
As you were the only one not getting paid.

This is One of Those

Poems in which the title is, in fact, the opening line.
And what appears to be the first line is really the second.
Failing to spot this device may result in the reader,
Unnerved and confused, giving up halfway through,

And either turning to another poem with a decent title
That invites him in, or (and this is more likely),
Throwing the book across the room and storming out
Into the voluptuous night* vowing never to return.

*'The Voluptuous Night', for instance, would make a decent title.

The Battle of Bedford Square

At a publishing party in Bedford Square
The critic is at ease
With lots of lady novelists
To flatter and to tease

He's witty, irresistible,
Completely on the ball
A few more wines, who knows,
He might make love to them all

But one by one they disappear
With a smile, and a promise to phone
And suddenly it's midnight
And suddenly he's alone

He surveys the litter, arty,
In search of a back to stab
Anger jangling inside him
Like an undigested kebab

Across the ashen carpet
He staggers, glass in hand
And corners a northern poet
Whose verses he can't stand

As if a bell had sounded
A space had quickly cleared
They were in a clinch and fighting
And the waiters, how they cheered

There was a flurry of books and mss
Bruises on the waxen fruit
A right to a left-over agent
Blood on the publisher's suit

A hook to a Booker Prize runner-up
A left to a right-wing hack
A straight to the heart of the matter
And the critic's on his back

An uppercut to an uppercrust diarist
From an anthropologist, pissed,
An Art Editor's head in collision
With a Marketing Manager's fist

Two novelists gay, were soon in the fray
Exchanging blow for blow
As the battle seeped into the Square
Like a bloodstain into snow

And though, at last, the police arrived
They didn't intervene
'What a way to launch a book.
Bloody typical Bloomsbury scene!'

All that now of course is history
And people come from far and wide
To see the spot where literary
Giants fought and died

Holding cross-shaped paper bookmarks
They mouth a silent prayer
In memory of those who fell
At the Battle of Bedford Square.

For the Sake of Argument

The cover of this book is yellow
But, for the sake of argument
Let us call it red.

It goes without saying that you are alive
But, for the sake of argument
Let us say you are dead.

And not only dead but buried
The headstone smeared with dirt.
(Don't take offence, it's merely polemic

You pretentious little squirt.
You self-regarding upstart
You couldn't write if you tried.)

So, for the sake of argument
Let's settle this outside.

*   *   *

Between the writer and the reader
Somewhere the meaning floats
And, waiting on the sidelines,
The poem holds the coats.

The Newly Pressed Suit

Here is a poem for the two of us to play.
Choose any part from the following:
    The *hero*
    The *heroine*
    The *bed*
    The *bedroom*
    The *newly pressed suit*
(I will play the VILLAIN)

The poem begins this evening at a poetry-reading
Where the *hero* and the *heroine*
Are sitting and thinking of making love.
During the interval, unseen
they slip out and hurry home.
Once inside they waste no time.
The *hero* quickly undresses the *heroine*,
carries her naked into the *bedroom*
and places her gently upon the *bed*
like a *newly pressed suit*.

Just then I step into the poem.
With a sharp left hook
I render unconscious the *hero*
And with a cruel laugh
Leap upon the *heroine*
(The cavortings continue for several stanzas)

Thank you for playing.
When you go out tonight
I hope you have better luck in your poem
Than you had in mine.

Framed

In the Art Gallery
it is after closing time
everybody has left
except a girl
who is undressing
in front of a large painting
entitled: 'Nude'

(The girl undressing
is the girl in the painting)

naked now she faces
the girl who gazes
out at the girl
who naked faces
the girl who
naked gazes out

of the picture
steps the nude
who smiles, dresses and walks away
leaving the naked girl
gazing into the empty space
Framed   by this poem.

the picture

In the Art Gallery it is nearly
closingtime. Everybody has left ex
cept a man and a younggirl
who are gazing at a picture
of themselves. Lifesize and life
like it could almost be a
mirror. However it is not a
mirror, because in a few minutes
a bell will ring and the man

and the younggirl will move
away leaving the original couple
staring into the empty space
provided by this   poem.

The Revenge of My Last Duchess

Downstairs, Neptune taming the sea-horses, let us descend.
The Count your master is generous and I seek his daughter's hand.

My first wife was put to death, at my command some say
I thought to reason with her, but that is not our way.

My name, after all, is nine hundred years old
She never appreciated that, and worse, her looks were bold.

Her eyes went everywhere and her smiles were cheap
Other men she whispered to, while moving in her sleep.

Bringing their lives, unwittingly, to an agonizing end.
Yes, even the painter of the portrait before which we stand.

Why do you ask? You pale. Why do you look alarmed?
A dagger raised? For pity's sake I an unarmed.

You cry vengeance. I beg, sir, what harm have I done?
Frà Pandolf! Oh God, I see him now, you are his son!

How Patrick Hughes Got to be Taller

Patrick was always taller.
In Bradford
when he drove a brick wall
and grew prize rainbows
he certainly was.

One of his secrets
is self-portraiture.
He draws himself
up to his full height
then adds a few inches
for good measure.

Another is his ability
to reduce the scale of objects
and people around him.

While friends and I
shrink into middle age
Patrick, cock-a-snook,
stands out like a tall thumb
on the nose of time.

Evenings I see him,
perspected against the bar
Full of *tromple-l'œil*
Beer in hand
Taller.

The Boyhood of Raleigh
After the painting by Millais

Entranced, he listens to salty tales
Of derring-do and giant whales,

Uncharted seas and Spanish gold,
Tempests raging, pirates bold.

And his friend? 'God, I'm bored.
As for Jolly Jack I don't believe a word.

What a way to spend the afternoons –
the stink of fish, and those ghastly pantaloons!'

Ex art student

Neat-haired and
low-heeled
you live without passion

hold down
a dull job
in the world of low fashion

ambition
once prickly
is limpid is static

portfolioed
your dreams
lie now in the attic

The Theatre

On arriving at the theatre in good time there was no queue
so I collected my ticket and passed through the empty foyer.
I bought a programme and called in briefly at the bar
before settling into my seat in the centre stalls.

I opened the programme to find that every page was blank
and was on the point of returning to the foyer to complain
when the house-lights began to fade. At that moment
I realized that I was completely alone in the auditorium.

But it didn't matter, because when the curtain rose
and the stage was flooded with light . . . nothing happened.
The only sound was the buzzing of the electrics
The only movement, the occasional ripple of the back-cloth.

Reluctantly at first I watched an empty space
thinking, I am watching an empty space. Then slowly
the emptiness within me began to fill the vacuum without.
Too soon the safety curtain like a dull screen-saver.

To avoid the usual crush I had taken the precaution
of ordering my interval drinks before the performance.
And alone in the bar sipped my whisky impatiently
until the first bell called me back to my seat.

Though similar in every respect, the second half
was even better than the first, and internalizing,
I could more easily interpret the significance
of what I was not seeing. The effect was dramatic.

When the final curtain fell I knew I had witnessed genius.
I jumped to my feet and applauded. 'Author!' I cried. 'Author!'
As the applause died down I climbed on stage, took a bow,
and with all due modesty, acknowledged the silence.

Big Ifs

To the mourners round his deathbed
William Blake was moved to say:
'Oh, if only I had taken
The time to write that play.'

Nor was William Shakespeare
Finally satisfied:
'I know there's a novel in me.'
(No sooner said than died.)

Beethoven in his darkest hour
Over and over he railed:
'If only I had learned guitar
Before my hearing failed.'

In the transept of St Paul's
Slumped Sir Christopher Wren:
'I'd give them something really good
If I could only do it again.'

Leonardo, Mozart, Rembrandt
Led sobbing through the Pearly Gates:
'If only I'd have . . .
I could have been one of the Greats.'

Children's Writer

John in the garden
Playing goodies and baddies

Janet in the bedroom
Playing mummies and daddies

Mummy in the kitchen
Washing and wiping

Daddy in the study
Stereotyping

Joinedupwriting

From the first
tentative scratch on the wall
To the final
unfinished, hurried scrawl:
One poem.

A Literary Riddle

I am
Out of my tree
Away with the fairies
A nut. A fruitcake. What am I?

Answer: one line short of a cinquain

What prevents a poem from stretching into Infinity?

what prevents a poem
from stretching into Infinity
is the invisible frame
of its self-imposed concinnity

Haiku

Snowman in a field
listening to the raindrops
wishing him farewell

Two Haiku

only trouble with
Japanese haiku is that
You write one, and then

only seventeen
syllables later you want
to write another.

The Spotted Unicorn

'Chi Wen Tzu always thought three times before taking action. Twice would have been quite enough.'

Having been an admirer of the great Chinese philosopher Confucius for many years, I was reading through Book 5 of the *Analects* (the choicest pearls of his wisdom) when I was suddenly struck by the above. Who was this Chi Wen Tzu? And what manner of man always reflected thrice before acting? My research led me to the discovery of a number of diaries written by an indecisive and yet inventive and brilliant poet, whose journal will shed surprising new light on a little-known period of ancient history.

8 October 480 B.C.

Tonight, young wife lying naked
on panda-skin rug. Full moon
hanging in sky like Chinese lampshade
(one of those round white ones).

At sight of fragrant body
its hills and valleys
bathed in silver light
am overcome with desire.

Wonder what course of action to take?

Make love, then and there?

Make tea, then make love?

Open bottle of rice-wine,
write up day's events in diary,
relax in warm bath,
then make love?

Wife gone home to mother for fortnight.
Not like being woken up at 4 a.m.
by drunken diarist.

Tonight, house cold and empty
as purse of K'ung Fu Tzu.

Have not eaten all day
so think about what to do for supper:

> *Send out for take-away?*

> *Drop in at Hard Wok Café?*

> *Crack open third bottle of rice-wine and see how feel later?*

[*Editor's Note*: No diary entries for several weeks.]

K'ung Fu Tzu (or Confucius
as now call himself) pop in
on way to Aphorism Conference.

Over dish of lapsang souchong
he relate long boring parable
about indecision and procrastination.

Fifteen minutes later
he repeat same parable.
Fifteen minutes later
heart sink as illustrious duffer
embark once more on inane ramble.

Consider three courses of action:

> *Feign bout of sleeping sickness?*

> *Allow to finish. He is, after all, old man; then laugh softly*
> *like moth alighting on moonlit breast of young wife?*

> *Interrupt?*

Interrupting, I say:
'Twice would have been quite enough.'

Innocent remark have strange effect
on esteemed Master
who jot it down on back of hand, rise up and go.

25 December

Nothing doing at home
so journey to mountains
to find cave in which to meditate.

All caves full.

China big country
and although many wise men
only so many caves.

Decide on course of action:

> *Transcend to higher astral plane?*

> *Descend to hire private plane?*

> *Give idea elbow and give young wife*
> *nice surprise on panda skin?*

31 December

Returning home along river-bank
pause to make water
against trunk of weeping willow.
Suddenly, on rickety bridge
see young wife in arms of Lin Fang!
Heart stop, turning off water.
End of rainbow spatter over feet
disturbing nesting ducks, who take flight.

Consider carefully what to do:

Kill wife?

Kill Lin Fang?

Design dinner service?

1 January 479 B.C.

Confucius call at humble home
on way to bamboo shoot.
Very apologetic about misbehaviour
of Lin Fang, favoured disciple.

Young wife enter, looking sheepish
(on all fours, going 'Baa, baa').
Everybody laugh, and Confucius
beg me forgive and forget.

Chi Wen Tzu reflect on three choices:

Forgive and forget?

Forgive now, kill later?

Have wife for supper with mint sauce?

2 February

T'ai Chi exercises interrupted
by owner of porcelain factory
who is much taken with design
for plates. Except for flying ducks.

He ask, why three different sizes?
I explain there is a daddy duck,
mummy duck and baby duck.
He nod, but go away unconvinced.

Wonder what to put in place of ducks:

Flock of budgies?

Swarm of locusts?

Pair of bluebirds?

Waking with sublime images in mind
arise and sit beneath mulberry tree
to compose poem for young wife.
It is entitled 'Poem for Ning'.

'Your eyelashes are like the finest willow-twigs
Your cheeks are whiter than the lily
Your teeth brighter than the scales
    of the Sacred Dragon
Your brow smoother than polished jade
Your body welcoming and transparent
    as a mountain stream.'

Deservedly pleased with poem, wonder whether to:

> *Show to young wife immediately?*

> *Put away until 2nd August and save
> money on birthday present?*

> *Change title and slip to exceedingly
> symmetrical daughter of factory-owner?*

28 *February*

Young wife try to appease husband
with gift of poetry book. Title?
New Generation Chinese Poetry.

Finding poems too long and impenetrable
decide to invent short, snappy verse-form.

With aid of abacus
Chi Wen Tzu ponder on its construction.

> *First, how many lines
> then how many syllables.
> Eureka! Haiku.*

[*Editor's Note*: Having invented the haiku, Chi Wen Tzu wrote several thousand
before going on to invent the sonnet, the villanelle, the limerick and the Malaysian

pantoum. The few that have survived illustrate the wide breadth of his poetic vision, and seem almost to pre-date some of the best-loved poems in English literature.]

There is some corner
of a foreign paddy-field
Forever China.

Wandering lonely
as cloud. Then heart leaps. Behold –
Golden pagodas!

On snowy evening
stopping by neighbour's dark woods
horse leaves steaming gift.

Sing of dappled things!
Freckled legs and pickled eggs
Budgies' wings. Nipples.

In forest of night
Panda! Panda! burning bright
Soon, bedroom carpet.

This is the night-mail
crossing the border. Oh no
Leaves on track – turn back.

If you can keep head
in time of Revolution
– you will be a man(darin).

Mongol hordes swoop down
on missionary and wife.
Noble six hundred!

Oh my luve's like red
red rose, pink, pink carnation
green, green grass of home.

Do not go gentle
Rage Rage Rage Rage Rage Rage Rage
Against lots of things.

Far out in cold sea
And not waving but drowning
Man see funny side.

           They mess you about
           Most honourable parents
           (But who gives a fuck?)

4 March

Young wife growing bored of late
which cause much concern
as memory of Lin Fang weigh heavily on loin.

Too much time on delicate but idle hand.

Confucius he say: 'Woman without hobby
like monkey brains without black-bean sauce.'

So husband choose suitable pastime:

    Buy her noodle-work kit?

    Acupuncture-repair outfit?

    Piano?

19 March

Hearing chopsticks on piano
enter music-room to find
young wife at keyboard
eating chow mein. Very angry.

Chew over possibilities:

    Chastise young wife?

    Part-exchange greasy piano
    for new young wife?

    Invent xylophone?

Form company to market
new line in tableware:
'Blue Willow Pattern, China'.

Chi Wen Tzu soon rich man.
Already orders flooding in
from all over country (like guests).

To celebrate good fortune, throw party.
Already guests flooding in
from all over country (like orders).

Tonight will be night to remember
but am nervous, so consider three choices.
Shall I:

      Assume lotus position and breathe deeply?

      Have sly puff on opium pipe?

      Hit plum brandy like no tomorrow?

21 April

Night to remember turn out to be
nightmare wish to forget.

Host, life and soul of party
until midnight, when am overcome
with urgent need to meditate.
Bathroom full, so stagger into garden
in search of willow-tree.

Hours later, awake in ornamental pond
to sound of birdsong and heavy breathing.
Filled with dark foreboding
creep behind pagoda, where, to horror,
discover young wife, naked with lover!

No time to consider three thoughts.
One thrust of sword through back
of Ling Fang dispatch sinful couple
to shamed ancestors.

Heavy of heart, kneel at pond
to wash blood from hands. Startled
by ghostly reflection of unicorn.
Turn suddenly. Nothing but shadows
and faint thirrup of echoing hoofs.

Pondering significance, walk back
to house to send guests home.
Imagine horror at sight of Lin Fang
crosslegged on floor
idly divining oracle bones!

Calm self to think three times:

> *Seek advice from Confucius?*
>
> *Identify corpse?*
>
> *Set fire to pagoda and head for hills?*

Decide on first course of action –
     But Confucius nowhere to be found.

Resort to second course of action –
     Confucius in first stage of rigor mortis.

Settle on third course of action.

Hills very pleasant this time of year
Orchids in full bloom
Distant sighing of temple bell
But winter reigns in kingdom of heart.

Nightmares of unicorn
galloping across rickety bridge
young wife, naked, clinging to flowing mane.
In sky above, pair of bluebirds
in eternal embrace
skewered by single arrow.
Drops of blood
          falling
                   into porcelain saucer
                            of moon.

Rabbit in Mixer Survives

A baby rabbit fell into a quarry's mixing machine yesterday and came out in the middle of a concrete block. But the rabbit still had the strength to dig its way free before the block set.

The tiny creature was scooped up with 30 tons of sand, then swirled and pounded through the complete mixing process. Mr Michael Hooper, the machine operator, found the rabbit shivering on top of the solid concrete block, its coat stiff with fragments. A hole from the middle of the block and paw marks showed the escape route.

Mr Reginald Denslow, manager of J. R. Pratt and Sons' quarry at Kilmington, near Axminster, Devon, said: 'This rabbit must have a lot more than nine lives to go through this machine. I just don't know how it avoided being suffocated, ground, squashed or cut in half.' With the 30 tons of sand, it was dropped into a weighing hopper and carried by conveyor to an overhead mixer where it was whirled around with gallons of water.

From there the rabbit was swept to a machine which hammers wet concrete into blocks by pressure of 100 lb per square inch. The rabbit was encased in a block eighteen inches long, nine inches high and six inches thick. Finally the blocks were ejected on to the floor to dry and the dazed rabbit clawed itself free. 'We cleaned him up, dried him by the electric fire, then he hopped away,' Mr Denslow said.

Daily Telegraph

'Tell us a story Grandad'
The bunny rabbits implored
'About the block of concrete
Out of which you clawed.

'Tell every gory detail
Of how you struggled free
From the teeth of the Iron Monster
And swam through a quicksand sea.

'How you battled with the Humans
(And the part we like the most)
Your escape from the raging fire
When they held you there to roast.'

The old adventurer smiled
And waved a wrinkled paw
'All right children, settle down
I'll tell it just once more.'

His thin nose started twitching
Near-blind eyes began to flood
As the part that doesn't age
Drifted back to bunnyhood.

When spring was king of the seasons
And days were built to last
When thunder was merely thunder
Not a distant quarry blast.

How, leaving the warren one morning
Looking for somewhere to play,
He'd wandered far into the woods
And there had lost his way.

When suddenly without warning
The earth gave way, and he fell
Off the very edge of the world
Into the darkness of Hell.

Sharp as the colour of a carrot
On a new-born bunny's tongue
Was the picture he recalled
Of that day when he was young.

Trance-formed now by the memory
His voice was close to tears
But the story he was telling
Was falling on deaf ears.

There was giggling and nudging
And lots of 'sssh – he'll hear'
For it was a trick, a game they played
Grown crueller with each year.

'Poor old Grandad' they tittered
As they one by one withdrew
'He's told it all so often
He now believes it's true.'

Young rabbits need fresh carrots
And his had long grown stale
So they left the old campaigner
Imprisoned in his tale.

Petrified by memories
Haunting ever strong
Encased in a block of time
Eighteen inches long.

*   *   *

Alone in a field in Devon
An old rabbit is sitting, talking,
When out of the wood, at the edge of the world,
A man with a gun comes walking.

Happy Ending

Out of the wood
at the edge of the world
a man with a gun
comes walking.
Feels not the sun
upon his face
nor hears a rabbit talking.

Over the edge
at the end of it all
the man stands
still as stone.
In his hands
the gun held
to his mouth like a microphone.

The rabbit
runs to safety
at the sudden cry
of pain.
As the man lets fly
a ferret
into the warren of his brain.

A Joy to be Old

It's a joy to be old.
Kids through school,
The dog dead and the car sold.

Worth their weight in gold,
Bus passes. Let asses rule.
It's a joy to be old.

The library when it's cold.
Immune from ridicule.
The dog dead and the car sold.

Time now to be bold.
Skinnydipping in the pool.
It's a joy to be old.

Death cannot be cajoled.
No rewinding the spool.
The dog dead and the car sold.

Don't have your fortune told.
Have fun playing the fool.
It's a joy to be old.
The dog dead and the car sold.

In Good Spirits

This icy winter's morning
I rise in good spirits.

On all fours I exhale
a long white breath
that hangs in the air
like a shimmering rope.

Under which, with arms akimbo
and eyes ablaze, I dance the limbo.

Nothing Ventured

Nothing ventured
I rise from my hangover
And take a walk along the towpath.

The wind is acting plain silly
And the sky, having nobody to answer to
Is all over the place.

The Thames (as it likes to be called)
Gives a passable impersonation of a river
But I remain unimpressed.

Suddenly in front of me, a woman.
We are walking at the same pace.
Lest she thinks I'm following her, I quicken mine.

She quickens hers. I break into a run.
So does she. It's looking bad now.
I'm gaining on her. God, what happens

When I catch up? Luckily, she trips
And sprawls headlong into a bed of nettles.
I sprint past with a cheery 'Hello'.

*　*　*

Out of sight, I leave the path and scramble
Down to the water's edge, where I lie down
And pretend to be a body washed ashore.

There is something very comforting
About being a corpse. My cares float away
Like non-biodegradable bottles.

A cox crows. The crew slams on its oars
And a rowing boat rises out of the water
To teeter on splintering legs like a drunken tsetse fly.

Before it can be disentangled
And put into reverse, a miracle: Lazarus risen,
Is up and away along the towpath.

Near Hammersmith Bridge, the trainer
Is on the other foot, as a hooded figure,
Face in shadow, comes pounding towards me.

A jogger? A mugger?
A mugger whose hobby is jogging? Vice-versa?
(Why do such men always have two g's?)

I search in vain for a bed of nettles.
No need. She sprints past with a cherry 'Hello'.
I recognize the aromatherapist from Number 34.

*　*　*

Waiting beneath the bridge for my breath
To catch up, I hear a cry. A figure is leaning
Out over the river, one hand on the rail.

His screaming is sucked into the slipstream
Of roaring traffic. On the walkway, pedestrians
Hurry past like Bad Samaritans.

I break into a sweat and run,
Simultaneously. 'Hold on,' I cry, 'hold on.'
Galvanized, I'm up the stairs and at his side.

The would-be suicide is a man in his late twenties,
His thin frame shuddering with despair,
His eyes, clenched tattoos: HATE, HATE.

My opening gambit is the tried and trusted:
'Don't jump!' He walks straight into the cliché-trap.
'Leave me alone, I want to end it all.'

I ask him why? 'My wife has left me.'
My tone is sympathetic. 'That's sad,
But it's not the end of the world.'

'And I'm out of work and homeless.'
'It could be worse,' I say, and taking his arm
Firmly but reassuringly, move in close.

'If you think you're hard done by
You should hear what I've been through.
Suffering? I'll tell you about suffering.'

We are joined by a man in a blue uniform.
'I can handle this,' I snarl.
'You get back to your parking tickets.'

He turns out to be a major
In the Salvation Army, so I relent
And let him share the intimacy of the moment.

I explain the loneliness that is for ever
The fate of the true artist,
The icy coldness that grips the heart.

The black holes of infinite despair
Through which the sensitive spirit must pass.
The seasons in Hell. The flowers of Evil.

*   *   *

The tide was turning and a full moon rising
As I lighted upon the existentialist nightmare,
The chaos within that gives birth to the dancing star.

I was illustrating the perpetual angst and ennui
With a recent poem, when the would-be suicide
jumped – (First)

The Sally Army officer, four stanzas later.
I had done my best. I dried my tears,
Crossed the road and headed west.

On the way home, needless to say, it rained.
My hangover welcomed me with open arms.
Nothing gained.

Days

What I admire most about days
Is their immaculate sense of timing.

They appear
inevitably
at first light

Eke
themselves out slowly
over noon

Then edge
surefootedly
toward evening

To bow out
at the very soupçon
of darkness.

Spot on cue, every time.

In Good Hands

Wherever night falls
The earth is always
There to catch it.

Bees Cannot Fly

Bees cannot fly, scientists have proved it.
It is all to do with wingspan and body weight.
Aerodynamically incapable of sustained flight,
Bees simply cannot fly. And yet they do.

There's one there, unaware of its dodgy ratios,
A noisy bubble, a helium-filled steamroller.
Fat and proud of it, buzzing around the garden
As if it were the last day of the spring sales.

Trying on all the brightest flowers, squeezing itself
Into frilly numbers three sizes too small.
Bees can fly, there's no need to prove it. And sting.
When stung, do scientists refuse to believe it?

My Life in the Garden

It is a lovely morning, what with the sun, etc.
And I won't hear a word said against it.

Standing in the garden I have no idea of the time
Even though I am wearing the sundial hat you gave me.

What the scene requires is an aural dimension
And chuffed to high heaven, birds provide it.

I think about my life in the garden
About what has gone before

And about what is yet to come.
And were my feet not set in concrete,

I would surely jump for joy.

The Perfect Place

The world is the perfect place to be born into.
Unless of course, you don't like people
or trees, or stars, or baguettes.

Its secret is movement.
As soon as you have stepped back
to admire the scenery
or opened your mouth
to sing its praises
it has changed places with itself.

Infinitesimally, perhaps,
but those infinitesimals add up.

(About the baguettes,
that was just me being silly.)

Happy Birthday

One morning as you step out of the bath
The telephone rings.
Wrapped loosely in a towel you answer it.

As you pick up the receiver
The front doorbell rings.
You ask the caller to hang on.

Going quickly into the hall
You open the door the merest fraction.
On the doorstep is a pleasing stranger.

'Would you mind waiting?' You explain,
'I'm on the telephone.' Closing the door to,
You hurry back to take the call.

The person at the other end is singing:
'Happy Birthday to you, Happy Birthday . . .'
You hear the front door click shut.

Footsteps in the hall.
You turn . . .

Here I Am

Here I am
getting on for seventy
and never having gone to work in ladies' underwear

Never run naked at night in the rain
Made love to a girl I'd just met on a plane

At that awkward age now between birth and death
I think of all the outrages unperpetrated
opportunities missed

The dragons unchased
The maidens unkissed
The wines still untasted
The oceans uncrossed
The fantasies wasted
The mad urges lost

Here I am
as old as Methuselah
was when he was my age
and never having stepped outside for a fight

Crossed on red, pissed on rosé (or white)
Pretty dull for a poet, I suppose, eh? Quite.

Uncle Roger

I am distinctly
ununclely.
I forget birthdays
and give Xmas presents
only when cornered.
(Money, of course, and too little.)

I am regrettably
ununclish.
Too thin to be jolly,
I can never remember
jokes or riddles.
Even fluff
my own poems.

My nephews and nieces
as far as I know
disuncled
me some time ago.
Better uncleless
than my brand of petty
uncleness.

Punk doll

Last week
I bought my favourite niece
A cute little doll
From a punk toy shop
In the King's Road.

When you twist the safety pin
In her rosy cheek
She vomits and shouts
'shitshitshitshitshit'
In a tinny voice.

The doll is pretty strange too.

Rocker-by

Hush-a-bye, Daddy, don't you cry
Baby will sing a lullaby

Your duck's arse
is thinning and grey
Your Elvis tattoo
is wearing away

Your bootlace ties
hang limp and frayed
Your 78s
are overplayed

Not rock 'n' roll
but aches 'n' pains
Drainies play hell
with varicose veins

Your blue-suede shoes
now have lead in them
Drunk each night
you go to bed in them
When the music stops
You'll be dead in them

Shush, old man, your day is done
Where mine has only just begun

Where It's At

I'm in the Health Club
I'm where it's at
Twenty minutes on the mat
Light circuit-training
Gentle jog if not raining
Sauna, jacuzzi
Sit by Suzi

I'm in the Wine Bar
I'm where it's at
Vino tinto into that
Pig out on tapas
Choose momento, make a pass
Scusi scusi
Chat up Suzi

I'm in the Porsche
I'm where it's at
Rocks off in Docklands' flat
Ecstasy, share a smoke
His 'n' hers, two lines of coke
CD something bluesy
Hold tight Suzi

I'm in prison
I'm where it's at
Didn't see the Passat. Splat!
Banged up on Isle of Wight
With terrorist and transvestite
Can't be choosy
Bye bye Suzi.

The Lottery

At five o'clock our time a killer was fried
According to law he was sentenced and died
Georgia the state where they favour the chair
When the switches were thrown I was washing my hair
Just lucky I guess.

At a quarter to midnight on his way to the shop
A stolen car hit him, revved up didn't stop
On arrival at Casualty he was found to be dead
When they rang up his wife I was reading in bed
Just lucky I guess.

At thirteen o nine it went out of control
The port engine failed and it started to roll
Imagine the scene on that ill-fated plane
When it burst into flames I was dodging the rain
Just lucky I guess.

At twenty fifteen it was 9, 24,
11 and 7, only needed three more
As each number came up I hardly could speak
Until I remembered . . . No ticket this week
Unlucky I guess.

Crazy Bastard

I have always enjoyed the company of extroverts.
Wild-eyed men who would go too far
Up to the edge, and beyond. Mad, bad women.

Overcautious, me. Sensible shoes and a scarf
Tucked in. Fresh fruit and plenty of sleep.
If the sign said, 'Keep off', then off is where I'd keep.

*   *   *

Midsummer's eve in the sixties.
On a moonlit beach in Devon we sit around a fire
Drinking wine and cider. Someone strumming a guitar.

Suddenly, a girl strips off and runs into the sea.
Everybody follows suit, a whoop of flickering nakedness
Hot gold into cold silver.   Far out.

Not wanting to be last in I unbutton my jeans.
Then pause. Someone had better stay behind
And keep an eye on the clothes. Common sense.

I throw another piece of driftwood on to the fire
Above the crackle listen to the screams and the laughter
Take a long untroubled swig of scrumpy. Crazy bastard.

Fear of Flares

I have this fear:
At a glittering occasion,
some kind of ceremony,
I am waiting in line
to be introduced to Princess Di
when I realize that I am wearing
flared trousers. Flared trousers!

There is no time to lose.
Unzipping them, I let them fall
around my ankles, then stand back
to attention. Her Royal Highness,
to her credit, makes no mention,
chats amiably, then moves on.
I pull them up. No harm done.

Q

I join the queue
We move up slowly.

I ask the lady in front
What are we queuing for.
'To join another queue,'
She explains.

'How pointless,' I say,
'I'm leaving.' She points
To another long queue.
'Then you must get in line.'

I join the queue.
We move up slowly.

Clutching at Cheese Straws

Out of my depth at the cocktail party
I clutch at cheese straws.
'Why are they called straws, do you think?'

Treading water, the ice-cool blonde
raises an eyebrow and shrugs.
'I mean, you can't drink through them.'

A second eyebrow reaches for the sky.
'Or is it because they taste like straw?'
A pause, and then she says:

'I assume it's the shape, don't you?'
Holding my breath, I take the plunge
and resurface with a crown of twiglets.

'Why are these called . . . ?' But she has been rescued.
Weighed down, I wade down to the shallow end
and help the lads keep aloft

A giant, inflatable hammer.

Half-term

Half-term holiday, family away
Half-wanting to go, half-wanting to stay
Stay in bed for half the day.

Half-read, half-listen to the radio
Half-think things through. Get up,
Half-dressed, half-wonder what to do.

Eat half a loaf, drink half a bottle
(Save the other half until later).
Other half rings up. Feel better.

Isolation

I like my isolation
Within easy reach of other people's
Wide-open spaces set me on edge
Than a bland savannah I'd rather be
Something clumped beneath a hedge

Perfume

I lack amongst other things a keen sense of smell.
Coffee I have no problem with. It leads me
by the nose into the kitchen each morning
before vanishing at first sip.

And cheap scent? Ah, bonsoir!
How many lamp-posts have I
almost walked into, senses blindfolded,
lost in the misdemeanours of time?

At twenty paces I can sniff the difference
between a vindaloo and a coq au vin.
Weak at the knees, I will answer
the siren call of onions sizzling,

Sent reeling, punch-drunk on garlic.
No, it's the subtleties that I miss.
Flowers. Those free gifts laid out
on Mother Nature's perfume counter.

Sad but true, roses smell red to me
(even white ones). Violets blue.
Everything in the garden, though lovely,
might as well be cling-filmed.

If I close my eyes and you hold up
a bloom, freshly picked, moist with dew,
I smell nothing. Your fingers perhaps?
Oil of Ulay? Nail varnish?

Then describe in loving detail its pinkness,
the glowing intensity of its petals,
and I will feel its warm breath upon me,
the distinctive scent of its colour.

Those flowers you left in the bedroom
a tangle of rainbows spilling from the vase.
Gorgeous. I turn off the light.
Take a deep breath. Smell only darkness.

5-star

The Mandarin Hotel, Jakarta.
5-star, bordering on the Milky Way.
Bathrobes a polar bear would kill for,
slippers I slide about in still.
A bowl with fruit so exotic,
you need a licence to peel,
and instructions on how to eat.
A bed as big as this room.

Attached to a cellophaned bouquet of flowers,
that looks too dangerous to unwrap,
a card from the Hotel Manager
who welcomes me (misspelling my name).
He telephones: Could we be photographed
together for the Hotel Magazine?
Puzzled, flattered and vaguely disquieted,
I agree. Within minutes
I am holding a glass of champagne,
his arm around my shoulder,
flicking through my limited series of smiles.

Then the inevitable: I am not
who he thought I was. I am not
who I am supposed to be.
He laughs it off, apologizes, and leaves,
taking the rest of the champagne with him.

I walk out on to the balcony.
From the 37th floor the city seeps
towards the horizon like something spilled.
Something not nice. That might stain.

I go back inside. Examine my passport,
and get out the photographs.
A couple who could be anybody
against a wall that could be anywhere.
A dog. Children smiling.

I unwrap the flowers. Open the maxi-bar.

Melting into the Foreground

Head down and it's into the hangover.
Last night was a night best forgotten.
(Did you really kiss a strange man on the forehead?)

At first you were fine.
Melting into the foreground.
Unassuming. A good listener.

But listeners are speakers
Gagged by shyness
And soon the wine has
Pushed its velvet fingers down your throat.

You should have left then. Got your coat.
But no. You had the Taste.
Your newfound gift of garbled tongue
Seemed far too good to waste.

Like a vacuum-cleaner on heat
You careered hither and thither
Sucking up the smithereens
Of half-digested chat.

When not providing the lulls in conversation
Your strangled banter
Stumbled on to disbelieving ears.

Girls braved your leering incoherences
Being too polite to mock
(Although your charm was halitoxic,
Your wit, wet sand in a sock).

When not fawning over the hostess
You were falling over the furniture
(Helped to your feet, I recall,
By the strange man with the forehead).

Gauche attempts to prise telephone numbers
From happily married ladies
Did not go unnoticed.

Nor did pocketing a bottle of Bacardi
When trying to leave
In the best coat you could find.

I'd lie low if I were you.
Stay at home for a year or two.
Take up painting. Do something ceramic.
Failing that, emigrate to somewhere Islamic.

The best of luck whatever you do.
I'm baling out, you're on your own.
Cockpit blazing, out of control,
Into the hangover. Head down.

Ode on a Danish Lager

The finger
enters the ring. A
pplause. Hooray!
Unzip.   A
pause. Then, whoosh,
The golden spray.

Unfurling slowly
like a blue mist
from a sorcerer's cave,
the genie is released
to serve a master
(soon to be slave).

A sip to mull over
the flavour
found only in the first.
I make a wish,
then slake
an imaginary thirst.

I squeeze the can
(it is not cannish),
is yielding, unmanish.
In it, my reflection,
modiglianish.

We wink at each other,
We're getting on well,
The genie weaves
his genial spell.

I unmask one more
(unheed the body's warning).
Goodnight, sweet beer,
See you in the morning!

Missed

out of work
divorced
usually pissed.

he aimed
low in life
and
        missed.

Used to Drink

Used to drink Pernod
Till my insides, an inferno
Said 'No'

Schooners of sherry
Soon as merry
Sick, very

So I drank rum
Yo ho ho as they come
Sore bum

What's nice is
Gin with lemon slices
Made me grin. Did me in

Turned to lager (Special Brew)
Went gaga
So will you

Downed tequila
Soon down at heel, ah
It's a killer

Odd dram of malt
Gave the old liver a jolt
Called a halt.

Mineral water
Herb tea
Beers (alcohol-free)
Cheers! I deserve a pat on the back . . .

(Next year maybe give up cocaine and smack.)

The Blues

Two a.m.
in the Blue Magnolia.
I smoke my last cigarette
and wait for the piano-player
to send me a drink over.

Star Juice

This morning
came a loud moaning
as a cloud
clutching its stomach
staggered across the sky
and threw up
all over Manchester

I know the feeling
It's been up all night
drinking with the moon
Star juice
It's a killer.

Drinking Song

Drink wine
Think romance
You're a lover

Feel fine
Sing and dance
Fall over.

Another Mid-life Crisis

3 a.m. Feeling like death
and wanting to end it all
I reach for the aspirin bottle.
Will there be enough?

One by one I count them out. 72?
Need more to be on the safe side.
Rummaging around I add another 30.
That should do it.

Take the first two with a glass of water.
Feel better. Go back to bed. Fall asleep.

Early-Morning Poems

(i)

Got up
did my toilet:
Washed
Shaved
Combed hair

My toilet looks much nicer now.

(ii)

Got up
Had shave
Did *Times* crossword

Had another shave.

Shavings Account

'Not to put too fine a point on it,'
Said the Bank Manager, pushing my finger
Into the desk-top pencil-sharpener,
'But you have a larger overdraft
Than I had given you credit for.'

He turned the handle. Turned the screw.
'Sorry, there's nothing we can do.
Business is business, we need our pound of flesh.
Next finger please. Put it in and . . . PUSH . . .'

Prayer to Saint Grobianus
The patron saint of coarse people

Intercede for us dear saint we beseech thee
    We fuzzdutties and cullions
    Dunderwhelps and trollybags
    Lobcocks and loobies.

On our behalf seek divine forgiveness for
    We puzzlepates and pigsconces
    Ninnyhammers and humgruffins
    Gossoons and clapperdudgeons.

Have pity on we poor wretched sinners
    We blatherskites and lopdoodles
    Lickspiggots and clinchpoops
    Quibberdicks and Quakebuttocks.

Free us from the sorrows of this world
And grant eternal happiness in the next
    We snollygosters and gundyguts
    Gongoozlers and groutheads
    Ploots, quoobs, lurds and swillbellies.

As it was in the beginning, is now, and ever shall be,
World without end. OK?

Fired with Enthusiasm

This morning
the boss
came into work
bursting
with enthusiasm

and fired everybody

In Case of Fire

In case of FIRE break glass
In case of GLASS fill with water
In case of WATER wear heavy boots
In case of HEAVY BOOTS assume foetal position
In case of FOETAL POSITION loosen clothing
In case of CLOTHING avoid nudist beach
In case of NUDIST BEACH keep sand out of eyes
In case of EYES close curtains
In case of CURTAINS switch on light
In case of LIGHT embrace truth
In case of TRUTH spread word
In case of WORD keep mum
In case of MUM open arms
In case of ARMS lay down gun
In case of GUN, fire
In case of FIRE break glass.

Vague Assumptions

I assume that the fire started before
    the fire-brigade arrived
I assume that the neighbours did not put on pyjamas
    and nightdresses to go out into the street
I assume that the woman is not in hysterics
    because the policeman has his arms around her
I assume that the suicide note left by the arsonist
    will not be found among the ashes

I assume that the siren's wail has nothing to do
    with the unhappiness of the ambulance
I assume that continentals drive on the right
    because foreign cars have the steering-wheel on the left
I assume that wing mirrors are a godsend
    to angels who care about good grooming
I assume that to a piece of flying glass
    one eye is as good as another

I assume that if the sun wasn't there for the earth to revolve around
    there would be fewer package holidays
I assume that a suitcase becomes heavy
    only when lifted
I assume that water boils
    only when the bubbles tell it to
I assume that because the old lady died
    the operation to save her life as a baby had not been successful

I assume that the bundle of rags asleep in Harrods' doorway
    is not queueing for the January sales
I assume that the people waiting in line for the DSS to open,
    do not work there
I assume that the people lying on the floor of the bank
    are not taking it easy
I assume that the hooded figure wielding a gun at the counter
    is not opening an account

I assume that to claim the reward
    one must hand over the kitten
I assume that the shopping-trolley on the beach
    has not been washed ashore from a deep-sea supermarket
I assume that to achieve wisdom
    one must arrive after the event
I assume that by the time you read this
    I will have written it.

It's a Jungle Out There

On leaving the house you'd best say a prayer
Take my advice and don't travel by train
As Tarzan said to Jane, 'It's a jungle out there.'

I'm not a man who will easily scare
But I'd rather lick maggots than get on a plane.
On leaving the house you'd best say a prayer.

Skateboards are lethal on top of a stair
A broken back means you'll not walk again
As Tarzan said to Jane, 'It's a jungle out there.'

When the sky turns purple better beware
Bacillus on the breeze and acid in the rain
On leaving the house you'd best say a prayer.

Avoid beef like the plague or your plague will be rare
Alcopops slowly eat away the brain
As Tarzan said to Jane, 'It's a jungle out there.'

Don't drink the water and don't breathe the air
For the sake of the children repeat the refrain:
On leaving the house you'd best say a prayer
As Tarzan said to Jane, 'It's a jungle out there.'

Flight Path (9/11)

A nice day for breakfast outside. Well-practised,
by now, birds sing out the end of summer.
On the wall, a marmalade sphinx, unblinking
doesn't miss a twitch in the garden.

In a hurry for Heathrow and bored,
a 747 scratches its dirty fingernails
down the clearblue, blameless sky.
We wince, the birds, the cat and I.

*   *   *

Across the pond, excited at the prospect ahead
they are up at first light and praying. The drive
out to Logan will be uneventful. At check-in
a girl will thank them and smile: 'Have a nice day.'

Don't Read All About It

He's there everyday on the corner,
the Bad News Vendor. The latest editions
hot off the press, the blood not yet dry.

The headlines scream again of murder.
A six-year-old girl. Part of a city. A small
civilization. In vain, he cries out:

'Don't read all about it! Don't read all about it!'

Survivor

Everyday
I think about dying.
About disease, starvation,
violence, terrorism, war,
the end of the world.

It helps keep my mind off things.

Everyday Eclipses

The hamburger flipped across the face of the bun
The frisbee winning the race against its own shadow
The cricket ball dropping for six in front of the church clock
On a golden plate, a host of communion wafers
The brown contact lens sliding across the blue iris
The palming of small change
Everyday eclipses.

Out of the frying pan, the tossed pancake orbits
    the Chinese lampshade
The water bucket echoing into the well
The black, snookering the cue ball against the green baize
The winning putt on the eighteenth
The tiddlywink twinkling toward the tiddlycup
Everyday eclipses.

Neck and neck in the hot-air balloon race
Holding up her sign, the lollipop lady blots out
    the Belisha beacon
The foaming tankard thumped onto the beermat
The plug into the plughole
In the fruit bowl, the orange rolls in front of the peach
Every day eclipses another day.

Goodbye bald patch, Hello yarmulke
A sombrero tossed into the bullring
Leading the parade, the big bass drum, we hear cymbals
    but cannot see them
One eclipse eclipses another eclipse.

To the cold, white face, the oxygen mask
But too late
One death eclipses another death.

The baby's head, the mother's breast
The open O of the mouth seeking the warm O of the nipple
One birth eclipses another birth
Everyday eclipses.

The End

What I love about everyday
        is the touch wood at bumping into one
What I hate about one
        is bone, the finger pointing towards death
What I love about death
        is the No, No, No, No it joyfully eclipses
What I hate about eclipses
        is that one extinction may encourage another
What I love about another
        is the hoary chestnut shared in the face of death
What I hate about death
        is the lack of rehearsal time to perfect one
What I love about one
        is lone, it begins and ends open-mouthed at birth
What I hate about birth
        is the back-log of stars it invariably eclipses
What I love about eclipses
        is the sure-as-eggs that one leads to another
What I hate about another
        is the alter ego we might have been at birth
What I love about birth
        is the universal surprise, on the dot, everyday
What I hate about everyday
        is The End, the beginning of eclipses.

The Bright Side

Things are so bad
I am reduced to scraping
The outside of the barrel.

And yet, I do not despair.
In the yard there are many
Worse off than myself. (Well, four:

A one-eyed rat
A three-legged cat
A corpse and the lavatory door.)

Worry

Where would we be without worry?
It helps keep the brain occupied.
Doing doesn't take your mind off things,
I've tried.

Worry is God's gift to the nervous.
Best if kept bottled inside.
I once knew a man who couldn't care less.
He died.

The Unknown Worrier

Don't worry, I'll do it for you
I'm a therapist *manqué*
Let me be your worry beads
I'll tell your cares away

Should I chance to sit beside you
In a café or a park
And a cloud is hanging over
Groaning, heavy and dark

You can bet that when it's time to go
You'll have nothing on your mind
While I sit in the shadow
Of the cloud you left behind

Don't worry, I'll do it for you
Relax, I'll take the strain
Anxiety is my forte
I've got worry on the brain

New Brooms

New brooms sweep clean
Old brooms can't be fussed
New brooms are mad keen
Old brooms can't stand dust.

New brooms are young bulls
Can't wait to get their teeth
Into the kitchen carpet,
Up the stairs and underneath

The fridge and the cooker
Where grease stains won't dissolve,
With each problem their bristles
Stiffening with resolve.

Old brooms are allergic
To dust and doggy hair
Than raise a whirlwind in the lounge
They would much prefer

To rearrange the particles
With a reassuring sweep,
Then lean against the cupboard wall
For a long and dreamless sleep.

'Dust is the carpet of the contented'
The motto of ancient brooms
And of the folk who sit contentedly
Waiting, in darkening rooms.

low jinks

today
i will play low jinks,
be commonplace.

will merge,
blend, change
not one jot.

be beige, be –
have, my friend
will fault me not.

couching myself
in low terms
i will understate.

today
i will give the little blue ones a miss,
and see what happens.

Passion

We keep our noses clean, my friend and i,
do what we're told.
Keep profiles soft and low
as we grow old.

We take up little space, my friend and i,
avoid the town.
Keep our curtains drawn
our voices down.

We live an ordered life, my friend and i,
cause little fuss.
If only everyone
could be like us.

*   *   *

Screaming now, he screams, my friend, and i
know what to do.
Have him put away.
(Well wouldn't you?)

Solarium

i own a solarium
and when it's cold
i simmer in
artificial gold

i keep away
from mornings grey
my private sun
smiles down all day

i pity those
whose flesh is white
as bronzed i sleep
alone each night

Dressed for the Occasion

I have enough jackets and trousers
Though shirts I may need to replace
A couple of suits I can oxfam
As they take up far too much space.

One overcoat, one jacket, leather,
One linen suit for summer weather
Hats of course, and a dressing-gown
Should last until the blind comes down.

Getting On

The husk may crack
The chalksticks creak
The brain confused
The pulse is weak

But Time is your own, at least
And that beast, Passion
No longer screams to be fed.

Getting Off

I closed my eyes, held my breath
and tried to lie quite still
Refused to believe that death
applied to me, until

You may get the vote at eighteen, but you're born with a price on your head

blue sierra
daguerreoscape
echo   echo
in some moonfilled canyon
as a rattlesnake
tosses in its sleep

Time to move on
I kick out the fire
and to the ground put my ear

He's still there
getting nearer year by hear.
The Bountyhunter
who knows my price
closing in.
White bones gleaming like dice
high heel boots
dusty
as sin

My Shadow is but a Shadow of Its Former Self

It was in Kalgoorlie last year, late one afternoon
the sun scorching my back, when, there at my feet
not a silhouette of anthracite, not a steam-rollered
Giacometti, but a gauze veil. A finely pencilled sketch.

I blamed the tinnies and thought no more about it.
But this summer, while jogging in Battersea Park,
I noticed that whenever I sprinted, my shadow fell behind
and I had to stop and wait for it to catch up.

I have also noticed that when the sunblock wears off
so does my shadow. Am I becoming translucent?
At midnight I play statues on the lawn. The moon
sees through me, but gives the cat a familiar to play with.

I fear that summertime when I will keep to the house
and feel my way around darkened rooms.
Dozing in armchairs, I will avoid the bedroom, where,
propped up on pillows and fading, waits my shadow.

Science, where are you?

I started smoking young. The Big C
didn't scare me. By the time
I was old enough to get it,
Science would have found the cure.

'Ad astra per angina' was the
family motto, and thrombosis
an heirloom I didn't care to inherit.
But I didn't worry. By the time
I was old enough to face it
St Science would surely have
slain that particular dragon.

Suddenly I'm old enough . . .
Science, where are you Science?
What have you been doing
all these years? Were you playing
out when you should have been
doing your homework? Daydreaming
in class when you should
have been paying attention?
Have you been wasting your time
and worse still, wasting mine?

When you left school did you
write scripts for 'Tomorrow's World'
before being seduced by a starlet
from a soap ad? Lured by the
bright lights of commercialism
did you invent screwtop bottles,
self-adhesive wallpaper, nonstick
pans, chocolate that melts
in the mouth not the hands?

Kingsize fags, tea-leaves in bags
beers, bras, voracious cars,
beans, jeans, washing-machines.
You name it, we buy it.

The Arts I expected nothing from.
Good company when they're sober
but totally unreliable. But
Science, I expected more from you.
A bit dull perhaps, but steady.
Plodding, but getting there in the end.
Now the end limps into view

and where are you? Cultivating
cosmic pastures new? Biting off
more Space than you can chew?
Science you're needed here, come down
and stay. I've got this funny pain
and it won't go awa
                        a
                            g
                               g
                                  h

Poem with a Limp

Woke up this morning with a
                                limp.
Was it from playing
                        football
In my dreams? Arthrite's first
                                arrow?
Polio? Muscular dystrophy? (A bit of
                                    each?)

I staggered around the kitchen spilling
                                    coffee
Before hobbling to the bank for
                                lire
For the holiday I knew I would not be
                                    taking.
(For Portofino read Stoke
                        Mandeville.)

Confined to a wheelchair for the
                                remainder
Of my short and tragic life.
                        Wheeled

On stage to read my terse, honest
                                        poems
Without a trace of bitterness. 'How
                                        brave.

And smiling still, despite the
                                        pain.'
Resigned now to a life of quiet
                                        fortitude
I plan the nurses' audition.
                                        Mid-afternoon
Sees me in the garden, sunning my
                                        limp.

*   *   *

It feels a little easier now.
Perhaps a miracle is on its way?
(Lourdes, w11.)

By opening-time the cure is complete.
I rise from my deck-chair:
'Look, everybody, I can walk, I can walk.'

Right as Rain

Alan's had his thingies done. You know, down there.
Hurt like hell at first but now he's fine.
He told us all about it in the bar.

The whole caboodle lasted half an hour.
Tied tightly with a sort of rubber twine
they drop off. Now Alan's right as rain. You know, down there.

Eighteen months ago he had a scare.
Blood in the pan was the ominous sign.
He told us all about it in the bar.

Unlike women, men don't really care
to talk about illness, it might undermine
the macho image. Especially when it's, you know, down there.

Making jokes about the bottom line
he gets them in, four lagers, two bitters and a dry white wine.
Alan's had this thingies done. You know, down there.
He told us all about it in the bar.

Say 'Ah!'

It hangs from the ceiling,
legs swinging. Zip
unfastening. My little grape.

Split uvula. Make a wish
and the palate is cleft.
Genetically a near miss.

A hair's breadth away
from a hare-lip
and thpeaking like thith.

Bits of Me

When people ask: 'How are you?'
I say, 'Bits of me are fine.'
And they are. Lots of me I'd take
anywhere. Be proud to show off.

But it's the bits that can't be seen
that worry. The boys in the backroom
who never get introduced.
The ones with the Latin names

who grumble about the hours I keep
and bang on the ceiling
when I'm enjoying myself. The overseers.
The smug biders of time.

Over the years our lifestyles
have become incompatible.
We were never really suited
and now I think they want out.

One day, on cue, they'll down tools.
Then it's curtains for me. (Washable
plastic on three sides.) Post-op.
Pre-med. The bed nearest the door.

Enter cheerful staff nurse (Irish
preferably), 'And how are you today?'
(I see red.) Famous last words:
'Bits of me are fine.' On cue, dead.

The Wrong Beds

Life is a hospital ward, and the beds we are put in
are the ones we don't want to be in.
We'd get better sooner if put over by the window.
Or by the radiator, one could suffer easier there.

At night, the impatient soul dreams of faraway places.
The Aegean: all marble and light. Where, upon a beach
as flat as a map, you could bask in the sun like a lizard.

The Pole: where, bathing in darkness, you could watch
the sparks from Hell reflected in a sky of ice. The soul
could be happier anywhere than where it happens to be.

Anywhere but here. We take our medicine daily,
nod politely, and grumble occasionally.
But it is out of our hands. Always the wrong place.
We didn't make our beds, but we lie in them.

The Health Forecast

Well, it's been a disappointing day
in most parts, has it not?
So, let's have a look at tomorrow's charts
and see what we've got.

Let's start with the head, where tonight
a depression centred over the brain
will lift. Dark clouds move away
and pain will be widespread but light.

Exposed areas around the neck and shoulders
will be cold (if not wearing a vest)
and there may be dandruff on high ground
especially in the west.

Further inland:
Tomorrow will begin with a terrible thirst.
Lungs will be cloudy at first,
in some places for most of the day,
and that fog in the throat
simply won't go away.
So keep well wrapped up, won't you?

For central areas the outlook is fairly bright
although the liver seems unsettled
after a heavy night,
and a belt of high pressure, if worn too tight,
may cause discomfort.

Further south it will be mainly dry
although showers are expected in private parts
and winds will be high,
reaching gale force incontinent.
Some thunder.

Around midnight, this heavy front
is expected to move in,
resulting in cyclonic highs
in and around the upper thighs.

Temperatures will rise
and knees may well seize up in the heat.
And as for the feet,
perspiration will be widespread
resulting in a sweaty bedspread.

And the outlook for the weak?
Not as good as for the strong, I'm afraid.
Goodnight.

In Vain

I like liposuction, I've had my lipo sucked.
No flab to grab on my abdomen
My buttocks neatly tucked.

Implants in my pectorals, wrinkles all erased
Nosejob and a hairpiece, both eyes doubleglazed.
Zits all zapped by laser, cheekbones smashed and reset.
But sadly, my days are numbered,
I'm up to my ears . . .
Remember how they used to stick out? . . . in debt.

(For in brackets here I'll mention
A certain *glandular* extension)
Penile, in fact, which increased my libido
Though senile I act like a beast
And the need, oh the greed,
Oh those nights of seedless passion!

Which will doubtless explain
The cardiovascular pain
And three-way bypass, alas, in vain.

Wearing pyjamas designed by Armani
A perfect body waiting to die.
Bewigged, butchered and bewildered
Am I,
        Am I,
                Am I.

THE ELEMENTS

Oxygen

I am the very air
you breathe
Your first
and last
breath

I welcomed you
at birth
Shall bid
farewell
at death

I am the Kiss of Life
Its ebb and flow
With your last gasp
You will call my name:
'o o o o o o o o'

Nitrogen

'O' is for Oxygen
so gregarious
whereas I am
colourless
odourless
and tasteless
unattractive you might say
unreactive in every way
nitrogen: the night
to oxygen's day

I am 75 per cent
of the air you breathe
so keep me clean
For when I latch on
to fumes that cars exhaust
I am poison
Nitro-glycerine
that's me as well   Dynamite
I can blow you all to hell

But I'm not without
a sense of humour
N_2O is the proof, nitrous oxide
Inhale some laughing gas
and see my funny side

N is my symbol
N for nebulous
necessary
and nondescript.

Carbon

I am an atom of carbon
And carbon is the key
I am the element of life
And you owe yours to me

I am the glue of the Universe
The fixative
used by the Great Model-maker
I play a waiting game
Lie low that's my secret
Take a breath every millennium

But though set in my ways
Don't be misled. I'm not inert
I will go down in cosmic history
as an adventurer
For when I do make a move
Things happen and fast

I am an atom of carbon
And carbon is the key
I am the element of life
And you owe yours to me

When the tune is called
I carry the message
to the piper
Take the lead
in the decorous dance
of life and death

Patient, single-minded and stable
I keep my talents hidden
Bide my time
Until by Time am bidden.

Iron

Fe fi fo fum
As hard as nails
As tough as they come

I'm the most important
Metal known to man
(though aluminium
is more common
do we need another can?)

Five per cent of the earth's crust
I am also the stone at its centre
Iron fist in iron glove
Adding weight to the system
I am the firma in the terra

Fe fi fo
Don't drop me on your toe

My hobbies are space travel
And changing the course of history
(they even named an Age after me
– eat your heart out Gold)

And changing shape of course
From axe heads and plough shares
To masks maidens and missiles
I am malleable
I bend to your will
I am both the sword and the shield
The bullet and the forceps

I am all around you
And more much more
You are all around me 2, 3, 4 . . .

You've got me
Under your skin
I'm in your blood
What a spin that I'm in
Haemoglobin
You've got me
Under your skin

So strike while I'm hot
For if I'm not there
What are you?
Anaemic that's what

Fe fi
High and mighty
Iron

Gregarious and fancy-free
Easy going that's me
No hidden depths

I'm not elusive
To be conclusive
You get what you see
Fe   Fe

Mercury

I repose at great speed
The joker in the pack
I cannot be fathomed
and turn your preconceptions
upside-down

You'll find me attractive
But I'm bad
(a poisoned chalice)
Hatters did
and they went mad
(ask Alice)

Alchemists
throughout the years
have been besotted by me
And understandably

I promised Gold
Immortality
The secret of eternal youth
What I delivered
was Death
A stab in the back
As befits
The joker in the pack

Quicksilver
I am a messenger
And the message that I bring
is . . .

Sulphur

I'm what gets witches
a bad name
Funny smells
Gobbledy spells
Given to theatrics
I go in for special effects:
Brimstone and treacle
Hellfire. Eureka!
Gold! The Elixir of Life! Immortality!

Chinese alchemists were obsessed
Emperors were impressed
But in Beijing
I couldn't stop them
– ageing
And so they died
(But not in vain)
For a potion more mundane
was chanced upon
The Chinese called it:
'Fire Drug'

Mobsters
got where they got with it . . .
Children
play a lot with it . . .
Cities
glow white hot with it . . .
Guy Fawkes
hatched a plot with it . . .

Gunpowder.

Gold

I'm not a colour
Let's get that one straight
right from the start
Sunsets   Daffodils   Eagles
All take my name in vain
For vanity it is
Let me explain:

I'm the heart of things   The core
The Emperor of metals
Hence, *or*
Without me, commerce
would grind to a halt.
No money   No trade
Civilization (as you wish to know it)
simply fade

Of course, I can bring out the worse
I admit
That people kill for me
That rivers of blood
have been shed in my name
But that's you   Not me.
I'm not to blame

I glister
Am all show   All style
My aim is simple
To make you smile

Come closer:
If you had gold
and were offered something else
Would you swap?
No
You see, I've every right to crow

Le Coq d'or
. . . The one on top

Fool's Gold

I'm not real gold
A sham
Pyrite is what I am

But I'm gold to the touch
And look like gold as well
So who can tell?

Except the scientist
(this alchemist who casts a spell
exposing me)
But I don't care
I had a good run for my money

Besides
All gold is fool's gold
For what is it after all?
Bright yellow dung?
The sun's tears?
Satan's urine?
Gold
All who love you are fools.

Element 109

A mayfly blinks
I have lived and died
a thousand times
Mine is a short life
but an exciting one
I am man-made
and owe my existence
to science
I have no name
merely a number:
109. It suits me.

I could go on
for hours and hours
about my various properties
But I won't

Now you see me
Now you . . .

Bob Dylan and the Blue Angel

What benign stroke of fate took Bob Dylan
to the Blue Angel Club after a gig at the Liverpool Empire
in 1965 remains a mystery. But there he was, seemingly alone,
all tousled up and shy, with Cilla goofing at the bar,
and Freddie Starr on stage downstairs.

Alan 'The man who gave the Beatles away' Williams
introduced us. 'He's a poet too.' So we talked poets and poetry,
music and lyrics, and soon we'd talked our way out of the club,
away from the noise and the crowd
and into the history of rock 'n' roll.

At the intersection of Bold Street and Hardman Street
he stopped. 'I'm at the crossroads, Rog,' he said.
'I can see that, Bob,' I said. 'No, I mean my career,
I don't know which way to turn.' 'Seems clear to me, mate,
let's have a coffee and I'll put you straight.'

So over cappucino in the Picasso I laid it all out.
Dump the acoustic. Forget the folksy stuff and go electric.
Get yourself a band. I remember the look on his face.
Sort of relief. The tension in the trademark
hunched shoulders seemed to melt away.

Hit the booze, make friends with cocaine
to get that druggy feel. Divorce your wife, the pain will pay off
in hard-won lyrics. His eyes closed, the bottom lip trembled.
Poet to poet, you asked for my advice.
I'm not here to give you an easy ride.

Ten years from now you'll be an icon. Sounds nice
but trust me, go against the flow. Dismantle the status.
Reinvent yourself. Embrace the faith of your fathers
then give Christianity a go. With nothing to lose
make albums that serve to confound and confuse.

Then consolidate. A Lifetime Achievement Award,
and then perhaps an Oscar. By the time you're sixty . . .
He smiled, 'Hold on there, boy, we ain't never
gonna grow old.' 'You're right, Bob.' We laughed
and made our way back to his hotel.

On the moonlit steps of the Adelphi
we exchanged phone numbers and addresses.
Suddenly he looked young and vulnerable.
Mumbling his thanks he hurried towards the entrance.
'Don't forget to write,' I called. But he never did. Never did.

Hey, Dude

Paul has probably forgotten about the incident by now
But I clearly remember that Saturday morning
In the sun-filled drawing room of his elegant home
In St John's Wood. His brother Michael and I
Relaxing over coffee and the morning papers
When he came bounding in like a young puppy.

'I've gorra new song, d'ye wanna hear it?' Needless
To say, we nodded and lowered our newspapers.
He was already at the baby grand. 'It's a gear tune,
But I haven't got the words sorted yet,' he explained
By way of introduction, and then began to sing:
'Hey, dude, get off of my cloud. *Dumpty dumpty*

Di dumpty three is a crowd *di dumpty dum di dumpty*
Dumpty dum Or I'll push you off like Humpty Dumpty.'
And so on and so on. And as the final chord faded
Michael and I made the required appreciative noises.
To have done otherwise would have seemed churlish.
'No, seriously,' he said, 'what do you really think?'

I knew from the way he was looking directly at me
That it was the truth he wanted. 'To be honest, Macca . . .'
I hesitated, but his eyes were begging me to continue.
'I think that the lyrics are working against the melody.
There's a lovesong in there, trying to get out, but . . .
Well, it sounds more like Jagger than McCartney.'

The reference to the Stones brought him to his feet.
To underline my point Michael sang the opening bars
Of 'Get off of my cloud' while his brother, head lowered,
Leaned against the piano as if his world might collapse.
I had to think on my feet, so I stood up and said,
'What about "Hey, Jude?" You know, use a girl's name?'

Paul looked puzzled. 'That's a funny name for a bird.'
'It's short for Judith,' I explained with all the confidence
Of someone having it off with a girl called Judith.
'Forget the dude. Forget pushing people off clouds.
Forget Humpty Dumpty. Think of the lovely Jude
And you've got another number one on your hands.'

He didn't say anything before going back upstairs
But the gentle squeeze of my shoulder spoke volumes.
As we left the house we could hear his guitar
As he unpacked his rich mind-hoard of love lyrics.
Outside, Michael and I selected a couple of the likeliest-
looking Beatles groupies and whizzed them down to the pub.

A Bolt from the Blue

In no way am I trying to lay claim
to kickstarting the career of Jimi Hendrix.
What took place that night might well have
happened anyway. But please hear me out.

The early sixties. At the Scotch of St James
in the heart of Mayfair, a meagre crowd
has turned up to witness Jimi's first UK
appearance. It was an embarrassment.

After the show, Chas Chandler came over
to ask if, as one of the only real celebrities there,
I would pop backstage to offer a few words
of advice and comfort to the young man.

Smaller in real life, he was languishing
on a velvet settee looking for all the world
like a black Little Lord Fauntleroy.
He groaned: 'I ain't never gonna play again.'

As I was about to protest, he picked up a cloth
and began to wipe the neck of his banjo.
It was then that I had the idea.
It came to me like a bolt from the blue.

Thank U Very Much

Taking a break from recording at Olympic Studios
the Gallaghers, large as life, were outside my local
that August evening, when, pen and notebook in hand
I strolled past as inconspicuously as possible.

But in vain. It was Noel who recognized me
and well-nigh dragged me over to their table.
Liam bought the round: red wine for his brother,
large whiskey for himself, and a lager top for me.

'Tell us about John Lennon.' 'Tell us about the Sixties.'
'Tell us about . . .' A double-act that was difficult
to penetrate. 'Relax, lads,' I said, 'well understand
your excitement, but one at a time, please.'

'Tell us about Scaffold.' 'Tell us about Brian Epstein.'
'Calm down, calm down,' I said with Aintree irony.
'If you're really interested, why not hit my web-site?'
Liam removed his shades.   'Gob-shite.'

My Divine Juggler

Jugglers, as you can imagine,
are great fun to be with.
Mine is.
Alert and ambidextrous,
rarely dropping an aitch or missing a trick,
head in the air, clear-eyed and smiling,
I'm mad for him.

No couch potato he.
After a hard day in the busy town square
he comes home to prepare supper.
Under the spotlight in the kitchen
he works the vegetables, eight at a time.
Spins plates, tosses pans.
In orbit, knives hiss with pleasure.

In the bathroom, ducks and deodorants
spring to life in his hands.
Loofahs loop-the-loop. A Ferris Wheel
of shower-caps and shampoo bottles.
Flannels paraglide, soaps and sponges
dance a perfumed fandango.
I would die for him.

He will be the perfect father, I know it.
In the maternity ward he arrived,
laden with champagne and flowers.
Matron gasped, midwives giggled,
other mothers marvelled as the newlyborn
went spinning through the air like startled planets:
Mars, Mercury, Jupiter. Our triplets.
My divine juggler.

Love Cycle

Up against the wall
Locked in passionate embrace
our two bicycles

M.I.L.T.

Blessed are the children and happy the spouses
Lucky the neighbours who everyday meet
Mothers In Leather Trousers

Pushing their buggies in T-shirts or blouses
Swish-swash hear them shimmying down the street
Blessed are the children and happy the spouses

Bricklayers' labourers stop building houses
Scaffolders, road-diggers, drivers compete
To whistle at Mothers In Leather Trousers

South Kensington ladies, Brummies and Scousers
Sisterhood of bottoms large or petite
Blessed are the children and happy the spouses

What a smooth and beautiful skin the cows is
Especially when softened and buffed up a treat
By Mothers In Leather Trousers

What man hasn't turned and tripped over his feet?
Polished anthracite with the promise of heat
Blessed are the children and happy the spouses
Who live with Mothers In Leather Trousers.

Echoes Sound Afar

Halfway up the mountain it stops. Slips back.
Judders. Slips again. *'Scheisse!'* screams a Fräulein,
'Scheisse!' Word for word, you think exactly
the same in English. Two little maids in white dresses,
toting Prada bags, think the same in Japanese.
The wind rocks the cradle, but not gently.

No driver. No door handles on the inside.
Reassuringly there is a hammer for smashing
windows in case of emergency. But is this
an emergency, or just the run up to one?
Unsure of the etiquette, better wait until the carriage
bursts into flames or fills up with water.

'Scheisse!' It slides back down the track.
Stops. Slides again. Stops and sways dizzily.
The German girl is on the floor sobbing,
her husband unable to comfort her.
A Texan, the life and soul, makes a joke
about the Big Dipper, but nobody laughs.

A voice crackles over the tannoy. *Pardon?*
If it were writing it would be illegible.
Why are there no Italians on board? Obviously
they've heard the rumours. So what did it say?
'Help is on its way', or, 'Emergency, you fools!
The hammer, use the bloody hammer!'

A power failure. Your lives hang on a thread
(albeit a rusty metal one circa 1888). A winch
turns and the long haul up begins. You hold
your breath. Twenty metres. Stop. Shudder,
and a sickening fall for ten. A tooth being
slowly drawn out and then pushed back in.

Should the cable break the descent will not be
death defying. The view below is breathtaking
but you have no wish to be part of it. Like the
muzzle of a mincing machine, the station waits
to chew you up and spit out the gristly bits
into the silver kidney bowl that is Lake Como.

An hour and a half later the tug-of-war ends
and the passengers alight heavily. The Brits to seek
an explanation. The Americans to seek compensation.
The Germans to seek first aid, and the Japanese,
seemingly unfazed, to seek a little shop that sells
snow-globes and model funicular railway sets.

Balloon Fight

'This morning, the American, Steve Fossett, ended his Round-the-
World balloon fight . . . I'm sorry, balloon "flight" . . . in northern
India.'

– *The Today Programme*, Radio 4, 20 January 1997

It ended in Uttar Pradesh.
It had to.
You can't go around the world
attacking people with balloons
and expect to get away with it.

What may be mildly amusing
at children's parties
in Upper Manhattan
will not seem so funny ha ha
on the Falls Road.

How Fossett fought his way
across the former Yugoslavia
I'll never know.
Some folk never grow up.
Hang on to their childhood.

Believing in the Tooth Fairy,
watched over by the Man in the Moon.
Thank you, Mr Newsreader,
for bringing him down to earth.
For bursting his balloon.

The Man in the Moon

On the edge of the jumping-off place I stood
Below me, the lake
Beyond that, the dark wood
And above, a night-sky that roared.

I picked a space between two stars
Held out my arms, and soared.

*   *   *

The journey lasted not half a minute
There is a moon reflected in the lake
You will find me in it.

Defying Gravity

Gravity is one of the oldest tricks in the book.
Let go of the book and it abseils to the ground
As if, at the centre of the earth, spins a giant yo-yo
To which everything is attached by an invisible string.

Tear out a page of the book and make an aeroplane.
Launch it. For an instant it seems that you have fashioned
A shape that can outwit air, that has slipped the knot.
But no. The earth turns, the winch tightens, it is wound in.

One of my closest friends is, at the time of writing,
Attempting to defy gravity, and will surely succeed.
Eighteen months ago he was playing rugby,
Now, seven stones lighter, his wife carries him aw-

Kwardly from room to room. Arranges him gently
Upon the sofa for the visitors. 'How are things?'
Asks one, not wanting to know. Pause. 'Not too bad.'
(Open brackets. Condition inoperable. Close brackets.)

Soon now, the man that I love (not the armful of bones)
Will defy gravity. Freeing himself from the tackle
He will sidestep the opposition and streak down the wing
Towards a dimension as yet unimagined.

Back where the strings are attached there will be a service
And homage paid to the giant yo-yo. A box of left-overs
Will be lowered into a space on loan from the clay.
Then, weighted down, the living will walk wearily away.

Sad Music

We fall to the earth like leaves
Lives as brief as footprints in snow
No words express the grief we feel
I feel I cannot let her go.

For she is everywhere.
Walking on the windswept beach
Talking in the sunlit square.
Next to me in the car
I see her sitting there.

At night she dreams me
and in the morning the sun does not rise.
My life is as thin as the wind
And I am done with counting stars.

She is gone she is gone.
I am her sad music, and I play on, and on, and on.

The Trouble with Snowmen

'The trouble with snowmen,'
Said my father one year
'They are no sooner made
Than they just disappear.

I'll build you a snowman
And I'll build it to last
Add sand and cement
And then have it cast.

And so every winter,'
He went on to explain
'You shall have a snowman
Be it sunshine or rain.'

*   *   *

And that snowman still stands
Though my father is gone
Out there in the garden
Like an unmarked gravestone.

Staring up at the house
Gross and misshapen
As if waiting for something
Bad to happen.

For as the years pass
And I grow older
When summers seem short
And winters colder.

The snowmen I envy
As I watch children play
Are the ones that are made
And then fade away.

In at the Kill

The contractions are coming faster now.
Every ten minutes or so
A crush of pain made bearable
Only by the certainty of its passing.

Midwives come and go.
At nine forty-five, a show.
It must go on. The floodgates open,
A universe implodes.

There is no going back now
(As if there ever was). Shall I slip away
And start a new life?
Instead, I do as I am told:

'Push, push. Stop, stop. Now push.
Come on, more. The head's coming.
Push harder. Harder. Push, push.'
Then out it comes – whoosh.

Uncoiled, I am thrown back.
For some reason I twirl.
Doubledizzy, I steady myself
On the bedrail. 'It's a girl.'

*   *   *

And so it is. My first.
Having witnessed three sons bawl into view
With the familiar appendage of their gender,
I am unprepared for . . . (what's the word,

Begins with *p* and ends with *enda*?)
Amazed, not by any lack or absence
But by the prominence of the lack,
The perfect shape of the absence.

Flashbulbs interrupt my musing,
The theatre fills with flowers.
My wife leads the applause,
I bow. 'Thank you . . . Thank you . . .'

Bearhugs

Whenever my sons call round we hug each other.
Bearhugs. Both bigger than me and stronger
They lift me off my feet, crushing the life out of me.

They smell of oil paint and aftershave, of beer
Sometimes and tobacco, and of women
Whose memory they seem reluctant to wash away.

They haven't lived with me for years,
Since they were tiny, and so each visit
Is an assessment, a reassurance of love unspoken.

I look for some resemblance to my family.
Seize on an expression, a lifted eyebrow,
A tilt of the head, but cannot see myself.

Though like each other, they are not like me.
But I can see in them something of my father.
Uncles, home on leave during the war.

At three or four, I loved those straightbacked men
Towering above me, smiling and confident.
The whole world before them. Or so it seemed.

I look at my boys, slouched in armchairs
They have outgrown. Imagine Tom in army uniform
And Finn in air force blue. Time is up.

Bearhugs. They lift me off my feet
And fifty years fall away. One son
After another, crushing the life into me.

Four Sons
(A Wish)

One son at each corner
of the bed
on which I lie

Four sons, the bearers
of the coffin
when I die

Just Passing

Just passing, I spot you through the railings.
You don't see me. Why should you?
Outside the gates, I am out of your orbit.

Break-time for Infants and first-year Juniors
and the playground is a microcosms:
planets, asteroids, molecules, chromosomes.

Constellations swirling, a genetic whirlpool
Worlds within worlds. A Russian doll
of universes bursting at each seam.

Here and there, some semblance of order
as those who would benefit from rules
are already seeking to impose them.

Not yet having to make sense of it all
you are in tune with chaos, at its centre.
Third son lucky, at play, oblivious of railings.

I try and catch your eye. To no avail.
Wave goodbye anyway, and pocketing
my notebook, move on. Someday we must talk.

Who are These Men?

Who are these men who would do you harm?
Not the mad-eyed who grumble at pavements
Banged up in a cell with childhood ghosts

Who shout suddenly and frighten you. Not they.
The men who would do you harm have gentle voices
Have practised their smiles in front of mirrors.

Disturbed as children, they are disturbed by them.
Obsessed. They wear kindness like a carapace
Day-dreaming up ways of cajoling you into the car.

Unattended, they are devices impatient
To explode. Ignore the helping hand
It will clench. Beware the lap, it is a trapdoor.

They are the spies in our midst. In the park,
Outside the playground, they watch and wait.
Given half a chance, love, they would take you

Undo you. Break you into a million pieces.
Perhaps, in time, I would learn forgiveness.
Perhaps, in time, I would kill one.

Cinders

After the pantomime, carrying you back to the car
On the coldest night of the year
My coat, black leather, cracking in the wind.

Through the darkness we are guided by a star
It is the one the Good Fairy gave you
You clutch it tightly, your magic wand.

And I clutch you tightly for fear you blow away
For fear you grow up too soon and – suddenly,
I almost slip, so take it steady down the hill.

Hunched against the wind and hobbling
I could be mistaken for your grandfather
And sensing this, I hold you tighter still.

Knowing that I will never see you dressed for the Ball
Be on hand to warn you against Prince Charmings
And the happy ever afters of pantomime.

On reaching the car I put you into the baby seat
And fumble with straps I have yet to master
Thinking, if only there were more time. More time.

You are crying now. Where is your wand?
Oh no. I can't face going back for it
Let some kid find it in tomorrow's snow.

Waiting in the wings, the witching hour.
Already the car is changing. Smells sweet
Of ripening seed. We must go. We must go.

Monstrance

He is neither big nor strong
But his four year old thinks he is

She runs towards him, arms outstretched
And is lifted up into the sky

Five times a week in Little Suburbia
He blazes like a tree

The Way Things Are

No, the candle is not crying, it cannot feel pain.
Even telescopes, like the rest of us, grow bored.
Bubblegum will not make the hair soft and shiny.
The duller the imagination, the faster the car,
I am your father and this is the way things are.

When the sky is looking the other way,
do not enter the forest. No, the wind
is not caused by the rushing of clouds.
An excuse is as good a reason as any.
A lighthouse, launched, will not go far,
I am your father and this is the way things are.

No, old people do not walk slowly
because they have plenty of time.
Gardening books when buried will not flower.
Though lightly worn, a crown may leave a scar,
I am your father and this is the way things are.

No, the red woolly hat has not been
put on the railing to keep it warm.
When one glove is missing, both are lost.
Today's craft fair is tomorrow's car boot sale.
The guitarist gently weeps, not the guitar,
I am your father and this is the way things are.

Pebbles work best without batteries.
The deckchair will fail as a unit of currency.
Even though your shadow is shortening
it does not mean you are growing smaller.
Moonbeams sadly, will not survive in a jar,
I am your father and this is the way things are.

For centuries the bullet remained quietly confident
that the gun would be invented.
A drowning surrealist will not appreciate
the concrete lifebelt.
No guarantee my last goodbye is au revoir,
I am your father and this is the way things are.

Do not become a prison-officer unless you know
what you're letting someone else in for.
The thrill of being a shower curtain will soon pall.
No trusting hand awaits the falling star,
I am your father, and I am sorry,
but this is the way things are.

INDEX OF FIRST LINES

INDEX OF SOURCES

After the Merrymaking (1971)

Gig (1973)

In the Glassroom (1976)

Holiday on Death Row (1979)

Waving at Trains (1982)

Sky in the Pie (1983)

Melting into the Foreground (1986)

Nailing the Shadow (1987)

Defying Gravity (1992)

Everyday Eclipses (2002)

Unpublished